MIND
UNDERLIES
SPACETIME

To Joy, Joe, and John

MIND
UNDERLIES
SPACETIME

an idealistic model of reality

by Daniel A. Cowan

Joseph Publishing Company
Box 770   San Mateo   California   94401

Library of Congress Catalogue Card Number 75–21384
International Standard Book Number 0–915878–01–1 cloth
0–915878–00–3 paper

Designed by Betty Barnes. Set in Optima, Palatino, and Aster typefaces by
Holmes Composition, San Jose, Calif. Printed in Berkeley, Calif. by
Consolidated Printers. Cloth binding by Cardoza-James, San Francisco.

Joseph Publishing Company, Box 770, San Mateo, Calif. 94401

Behind the tireless efforts of the investigator there lurks a stronger, more mysterious drive: it is existence and reality that one wishes to comprehend.

Albert Einstein

The eternal God is thy refuge, and underneath are the everlasting arms.

Moses

All is infinite Mind and its infinite manifestation.

Mary Baker Eddy

Contents

Preface

Philosophy is our search for the largest reference frame in which we can locate our interests, delights, and concerns. Not a sudden effort, it is rather an almost unnoticed activity in which you and I constantly engage. Whether we do it with intellectual honesty and humility or merely from feelings of cleverness, our outlook still influences our lives. Whenever we are noticing more of the overall scheme of things we are doing philosophy; and if our gaze is gradually lifting above the ephemeral or merely personal to appreciate larger, more enduring patterns, then likely we are doing philosophy well.

Honesty in philosophy demands that we be willing to dig deep as well as to climb to the higher, wider view. Through our philosopher eyes we find hidden premises behind our view of justice. In the field of medicine we can't help but confront our concept of health and life. In commerce we eventually come face to face with our sense of value and self-respect,—in education, with our concept of man. In the sciences we ultimately ask what is substance and what are the foundations of consciousness and reason. On the whole, it would seem that all these subjects must be related if they are occurring within the same universe.   But how are they related?   What is the abiding reference frame?

Were it not that I am writing about this framework or underlying principle, I should hardly dare offer a theory that affects the foundations of so many different disciplines. Primarily, this theory seeks to show that space and time are not external to consciousness. It does this by seeking to show how our finite-appearing universe can be accounted for from the basis of an *infinite system* that is totally mindlike. Down through the ages the main question of philosophy has centered on whether or not matter is the basic substance behind the universe's existence. Recently, theoretical physicists have shifted this question toward asking whether spacetime structure—the dynamic spacetime geometry thought to underlie matter—is the basic substance. But the ultimate scientific question goes even deeper because men and women still feel impelled to look for a spiritual dimension to life. The deepest question from the scientific point of view is whether the basic substance is *finite* or *infinite.* (These terms will need to be elucidated, of course.)

The theory presented in this book hypothesizes an infinite system unlike anything that previous idealistic philosophers have proposed. Especially is it unlike the various straw-man systems that materialists frequently set about demolishing—so-called idealistic systems that are variants of Berkeley's 18th century empiricism. Such systems turn out to be as finite as most versions of materialism.[1]

One normally would expect it quite enough for a new theory to touch the uncertainty principle in quantum physics and the "geometry," "superspace," and "pre-geometry" of contemporary relativity theory. But to have it also propose a solution to the age-old mind-body problem—or the more recent mind-brain identity theory—may seem downright audacious. One can, however, hardly attempt the most basic philosophical redesign in any one of these areas without jostling the theoretical structure of many disciplines. I view the theory in this book as even going deep enough to provide a general foundation for psychology. The theory has even led the author into the foundations of mathematics and set theory (to what, so far, seems a solution to a major problem in axiomatic logic brought on by Gödel's rather famous theorem on the incompleteness of rich axiom systems). Fortunately for the reader, this latter subject is confined almost entirely to the Appendix.

More important than any of the above, it is my hope that this book details a scientifically acceptable link between the vision of religion and that of science—a link that goes beyond mere tenuous faith. When faith is used as the corner stone, it often turns out to be blind faith enthralled by ignorance masquerading under an aura of mystery. Life always will be full of wonder and discovery, but mere mystery for mysticism's sake seems to be the "press-agentry" we use to entertain ourselves or urge the rearrangement of each other's lives. The true sense of mystery and wonder should spur us to discover how marvelously arranged the universe actually is. But, before mankind can advance a great deal further in understanding the universe or the ultimate link between science and religion, the sciences need an encompassing theory for dealing with what is too often regarded merely as man-made value judgments—such traits as honesty, truth, love.

One of the aims of this book is to revise radically our deep-rooted concept of spacetime as external and prior to consciousness. This old concept is exercising considerably more influence in our lives than we tend to realize. Men and women are today ready for better explanations of identity, expression, and self-control and are looking for a concept of man[2] that takes into account the spiritual dimension. Yet the concept of a finite universe framing life is hindering this advance. People want to deal intelligently with today's opportunities concerning the quality of life, home and family, education, work, medicine, and religion. Our concept of living within a spatio-temporal system is deeply involved in each of these issues. It must sooner or later be dealt with if we are to obtain a better handle on life and existence.

A personal reference would normally be out of place in an attempted scientific theory; but because this particular theory argues that the ultimate framework or Principle can properly be called God, the reader is entitled to know what point of view the author brings to this issue. My own religious persuasion is that of a Christian Scientist. I am, however, not trying to promote religion—other than by urging a deeper appreciation of the Bible. Both the Bible and the book *Science and Health with Key to the Scriptures* by Mary Baker Eddy have played a significant role in directing my inquiry. Religious talk, however, has been left out of this presentation except for a few Bible quotations which even the most ardent religious skeptic might forgive.

The first three chapters of the book are introductory and are not part of the formal theory, but they help the reader to grasp the new point of view presented. Chapter four presents the hypothesis for the infinite system set forth in seven informally stated axioms. Chapters five and six present a deductive argument based on the axioms that seeks to account for the finite appearances we so readily apprehend. Chapter seven suggests an approach toward designing a laboratory test of the hypothesis. The reader may do best by reading all seven chapters (and the Appendix if he is so inclined) through once rather quickly before beginning a detailed analysis of any particular point or of the notes at the end of the book. An overall perspective is as necessary in achieving a detailed understanding of specific points as is the reverse.

This edition is presented with the hope its readers will offer the author sufficient helpful comments to warrant revision and expansion of the book.

Acknowledgements:

Many people have played a part in the unfolding of this research project over the past four years. Their suggestions and comments have been of great help to the author. Especially I wish to thank Professor John Burke for his helpful comments on chapter three and Professor Craig Harrison for his constructive criticism of an early draft of the Appendix. And for their editorial suggestions and assistance I owe much gratitude to John Cuno, Mary Lou Maxson, David Salisbury, Jeremy Carper, Barbara Wyman, and to my wife's parents, Chester and Dorothy Bemis. Most of all, this adventurous journey has been aided by the steadfast help and encouragement of my wife, Joy.

D.C.

San Mateo, August 1975

1 Toward Clearer Views of Existence

The universe is happening, and you and I are involved in what is happening. While humans are carefully describing many of the universe's unfolding details—attempting to understand its vital processes—are we humans looking in the right direction to understand what is basically happening? Our leading scientists do not yet agree on the fundamental nature of matter and energy and thus are reluctant to address broader, philosophic questions about existence, substance, change, and causation. Psychologists hold such varied and conflicting views about consciousness and about what is happening when you and I think and feel, that they are the more divided over what gives purpose and meaning to our lives. Some philosophers even discourage a search for ultimate answers. They question whether anyone knows what kind of behavior properly counts as criteria for a fundamental understanding of existence. Meanwhile, religionists find popular faith surging or slackening according to the currents and satisfactions of the times.

In all these areas of question, one dominant view influences humanity's attempts to think through to the basics. This view holds that an understanding of existence amounts to getting our thought processes and language co-ordinated in some useful way with the behavior of an external world framed and shaped within space and time. This so-called "real world" is generally considered to consist of physical forces and impersonal events exterior and anterior to anything resembling thought. I suggest that this view is faulty. Up to now, it has been a useful view because it has represented a step beyond animism—the primitive belief that nature is controlled by capricious spirits. Nevertheless, the view is becoming increasingly inadequate to meet our growing need for a more useful and holistic concept of existence and life's capacities.

There are reasons to doubt that any kind of existence can be ultimately external to consciousness—provided the term 'consciousness' is adequately defined. Even our present dim sense of this word 'consciousness' is likely to convey a more accurate impression of the framework of the universe than do the present scientific-mathematical notions about spacetime. Putting this differently, there are good reasons to believe that the observable, material world is a composite mental event rather than an event framed in a spacetime that is actually "out there" on its own. While "physical" events are obviously much more objective than fantasies and dreams, yet, according to the theory I am advancing, even physical events and their spatio-temporal structure are totally mental. They are subjective in respect to a "larger" mental structure which frames not only animal and human consciousness but all rocks, winds, and atoms as well.

Perspective

For a bit of perspective, consider how this vast universe of ours seems to extend endlessly outward—on and on into the void. Its estimated ten-thousand-million other galaxies (the largest of which contains at least a quarter-trillion stars) are reeling and sprawling across an expanding space whose boundaries are receding from our own galaxy (the Milky Way) with almost the speed of light. These outer bounds, we are told, are more than eight billion light years beyond the farthest reaches of our Milky Way—which itself contains roughly 100-billion sun-stars plus an immense host of planets.

Now, let's switch our view down to the smallest details of the universe. We can well be amazed that the same immensity extends into this realm. For here, within say the miniscule dot ending this sentence, we are told there are millions of molecular systems. Their constituent atoms each encompass even vaster subsystems as we press inward toward the strange subnuclear world of quantal energies and infinitesmals.

Again switching our view, consider how the extremes in vastness extend into the dimension we call "time." Here, the scientist deals accurately with relationships involving a few one-thousandth-millionths of a single second on the one hand and with processes spanning billions of years on the other. But all this vastness—the macrocosm and microcosm, the accumulating eons and the millionth part of a moment—all this may not exist outside of a certain thought process underlying mortal experience. Though we realize it not, we may be very much involved in what is happening "everywhere." Mankind's discovery and understanding of this possibility could be as near as thought itself.

Portentous changes in our understanding of the ordinary loom at us from every horizon. The common notion that we are dwellers within a largely unconscious, yet astoundingly dynamic* spatio-temporal universe may already be yielding to the new-old idea that space and time are really conceptual experiences—constructs of our type of incomplete awareness. Albert Einstein was possibly alluding to such an idea when in 1955 he wrote to the bereaved family of a close friend with whom he had corresponded for more than fifty years, "For us believing physicists, the separation between past, present, and future has only the meaning of an illusion, albeit a tenacious one."[1]

A Different System

It is my contention that the fundamental nature of the universe can be described, once we get beyond the notion that our description must involve quantitative measurements (such as meters and microseconds). The universe needs to be recognized as a different kind of system—an infinite system. Such a system is comprised of what philosophers would call "universals." Universals, as I speak of them, are the attributes of a single, mindlike substance. These attributes are, in a manner of speaking, larger than the largest finite measurement and smaller than the smallest. Being both infinite and infinitesmal, they utterly swallow up comparison with finite impressions. And yet, finite impressions are relatable to these universals in a way that we will trace in chapters five and six. My hypothesis that these omnipresent qualities actually exist will be developed in chapter four. Suffice it to say now that these attributes—spiritual attributes if you will—are related to elements of our own thinking,

---

*Consider the dynamic expansion of the universe and the equally dynamic collapse of giant, burned-out stars into "black holes."

although human thought is neither their cause nor their source. The primary relationship is direct, but there are also inverse relationships. Consequently, there are combinations of direct and inverse relationships. The way in which this happens is roughly sketched in the following three paragraphs.

To begin with, 'thought' is the broad term encompassing our diverse mental landscape—a panorama ranging all the way from dark swamplands of fear and despair, through more hospitable country of reason, hope, sorrow, and joy, on into the highlands of artistic, intellectual, and spiritual discovery and enlightenment. I hope to show how all of this mental scenery is composed of bedrock spiritual qualities in combination with something remarkable, namely, the *seeming absence* of these very same qualities. *This combination of universal "building blocks" with their specific seeming absence is the key to this theory.* It can account for our impression of finite existence within a finite universe. The permanent elements of experience, according to this theory, are the attributes of the infinite substance, while their seeming absence is the negative or opposite of the attributes. How this process accounts for the material world we see about us is the main point of this book.

Analogy of this Theory

In brief, this book sets forth the explanation that matter is a phenomenon resulting from the way our thought focuses to create an incomplete level of awareness. This mental process is hinted at in the following physical analogy. Consider how you observe the black print on this page. For practical purposes, all that the eye actually "sees" is the white light surrounding the black letters (since the black represents the absence of visible light).

And yet you keep focusing your attention on the empty places where you see nothing—instead of on the surrounding white background that you do see. In other words, you read black print by noticing the sharp *contrast* between "not seeing" and "indirectly seeing" (not seeing the foreground and indirectly seeing the background). This amounts to noticing an arrangement of holes—holes in light—just as if holes were real objects of themselves.

If we carry this analogy of focusing on "holes" over to the mental realm posited by this theory, we find an amazing effect. Its explanation can provide the missing link in the understanding of consciousness and its relationship to experience.

We will first need to define what is meant by "being conscious of a quality" and by "being conscious of the contrast caused by its apparent absence from one's awareness." We will then consider the *inversion* of such a contrast. This is in order to understand how mental inversions, multiplied a thousandfold, can significantly affect one's unobserved mental state. The process shifts one's recognition from an infinite base over to a preponderance of incomplete views suggesting that individual identity is temporary.

Idealistic Philosophy

I hope that the foregoing quick overview has indicated to the reader new terrain worthy of step by step exploration. The terrain is surprisingly primitive in spite of philosophy's long history of adventuring into almost every conceivable type of metaphysical landscape. Idealistic* philosophers have long searched for the promised land of ontological reality, and they have experi-

*Idealistic philosophy is so named because it treats ideas as primary reality.

enced horrendous difficulties, if not downright failure, in attempting to find an idealistic system that is internally consistent and still able to hook up with the observable world. Because of these difficulties, idealism has been in disfavor with Western philosophers for more than three decades. And yet, the present emphasis on non-idealistic, materialistic theories commits mankind to assuming that existence must be founded within the framework of finite spacetime. This assumption may be as shaky as the proverbial house built on sand.

Must Science Presuppose Finiteness?

Most scientific explanations presume that space and time are essential to existence—certainly to life and consciousness. Scientists who accept such a premise quite logically arrive at materialistic conclusions. But the assumption that science *must* premise its activities upon the concept of finite reality is only an assumption. The real spirit of science is to discover those trustworthy aspects that give existence its order, harmony, and intelligible cohesiveness. Logic and mathematics are its handmaids, and they are not finite in any immediate physical sense. Finiteness is not essential to the clarity that scientific thinking prizes; finiteness is a mode of expression,—but how adequate or inadequate has not yet been widely understood. This book shows how finiteness is a faulty interpretation of an infinite basis that is preeminently tangible.

Furthermore, this book shows how our continual materialistic interpretation of the deeper order behind genetics, environmental conditioning, and physiological stimuli is molding our "scientific" conclusions into a faulty model of existence. One of the effects of science that restricts itself to drawing conclusions from only finite presuppositions about substance is that it discourages our innate faith in the intelligibility of life and its undergirding forces. This discouragement causes popular thought to rebel and swing to the opposite extreme of mysticism. People begin to believe that science can show them no other framework for their existence than a strictly finite, materialistic framework.

Clarification

It might help if I clearly state that the theory in this book does not describe consciousness as a characterization of cybernetic processes in the left and right hemispheres of the brain. There has been much recent interest in the theory that rational abilities are related to one side of the brain while intuition stems from the other side. My theory bears directly on this subject, but it does not start with the brain or hold that consciousness comes from the brain. Nor is it an attempt to explain how knowledge results from our working-over the raw materials furnished by our physical senses. Rather, this theory argues that a framework of consciousness (and not a physical universe) is the necessary precondition for the appearance of physical sense—not merely for humans but even for the simple amoeba.

This idealistic theory is, first, a theory of how individual consciousness is the effect of one Mind to which we can properly apply the name 'God' (in the tradition of this name representing the Principle behind all life and intelligence). Second, it is an explanation of how hypothetically incomplete views within consciousness interact to produce our human experience and its material universe—with our awareness seemingly imprisoned inside.

Before launching into the details, let us look briefly (chapters two and three) at the problems inherent in attempts to describe what is happening from a materialistic view. We need to see how the materialist's unsolved problems (as well as the idealist's unsuccessful attempts at solving them) are related to his presuppositions about space and time.

2 What is Meant by 'Reality'?

Changing Meaning at Each Level of Abstraction

Humans, it seems, have always philosophized about life and existence, and yet many of the great philosophical questions have stubbornly resisted solution. The lack of success in agreeing on man's nature and basis has persisted in spite of the feeling that absolute truth does exist; and it persists in spite of the almost contrary conviction that the physically tangible universe is the ultimate reference for deciding all claims of truth.

But philosophers today are ready to point out at least one reason why these puzzles have resisted solution. The great questions have not been stated and analyzed within any one consistently held level of meaning. Such questions generate confusion when their words have long been used at two or more levels of abstraction[1]—levels

whose relationship to each other is not clearly understood. And discussions become downright muddles when,
midway, people unintentionally switch their levels of
abstraction. Furthermore, questions asked in respect to
the largest possible context usually involve such slippery
concepts as reality, life, truth, and existence, and frequently such often-vague words as 'freedom,' 'goodness,'
'beauty,' and the like. These are the words and concepts
that readily operate at more than one level of abstraction; and within each level they begin to be associated
with the view of reality as seen at that level.

The Word 'Existence'

Consider the word 'existence.' Notice how we speak of the
existence of not only particular things like the
Washington Monument but also of general things as in
saying "water exists in milk." We also speak of the
existence of intangibles like the law of gravity, the law of
the excluded middle, and the law of treating others as
you would hope to be treated. Naturally, we tend to think
of some of these types as having a more basic existence
than the others and that the others are therefore abstractions from a basic level. But, because we are influenced
by our present, possibly narrow point of view, we pre-
judge which level is basic. We favor meanings that relate
to our most noticeable type of experience. Then, when we
examine something that is less-immediately tangible
(such as an idea), we tend to judge its reality by our
standard for, say, sensations or physical objects. It is as
though we are carrying an analogy too far.

What we are talking about in the case of the word
'exist' is the subtle assumption that it implies "having
being in space and time" instead of *having being*. This
further implies that to exist is to have finite existence. Of

course, the ordinary assumptions of existence in spacetime are often convenient in the same way a simplified view of the earth as flat is convenient for navigating around town or a view of the sun as traveling westward is convenient for figuring out where to plant a shade tree. But for more comprehensive activities such as space travel, we need to at least picture the earth as spherical and rotating eastward rather than the sun as sailing west. Likewise, in thinking about the long-run solution to some problem, we should not automatically adopt the usual convenient assumption that life's structure is necessarily captured within spacetime. This assumption may well be what keeps us from really understanding some important aspect of life such as the meaning of honesty. We avoid this trap if we use 'existence' to mean "having the same degree of reality as the largest context with which we are immediately concerned."[2]

Although these conclusions are not quite the same as reached by Ludwig Wittgenstein at Cambridge a few decades back, yet he did call attention to the philosophical problems relating to our use of words. He imaginatively described what he called "language games"[3] we humans unwittingly engage in when we confuse meanings through their different levels of use. The confusion is harmless—until we try to answer the broader, philosophic questions about what is happening.

Let us quickly examine several cases where a different implication is taken on by a word at each level of abstraction.

First, look at the word 'first.' Commonly it refers to that which is occurring earliest in time or at some arbitrary starting place in space. When qualities are more in view, it means the best. Mathematically, it is the ordinal number for the cardinal number "one." At still another level it means *fundamental* as in "first cause." If someone is discussing the possibility that there is a first cause called God, and he unconsciously assumes that the first cause is the temporally prior cause, then he has already confounded his argument. He is accepting time itself as his first cause, even though he believes he is arguing for God in this role. Such unrecognized confusions have muddled debates over God's existence for centuries.

Consider the words 'I see' in their literal and figurative sense. Semanticists properly conclude that both uses stem from the same original activity. But they should not fall into the unproven assumption that that original activity was necessarily one of physical impressions. This conclusion would follow only if we are given the *a priori* knowledge that reality itself is fundamentally physical.

'Truth'

Consider the word 'truth.' When we speak of "the truth," we are usually confining our remarks within an implied context. Suppose we have a friend who is much given to philosophical musing, and he is summoned as a witness in court. After he is duly sworn to tell the *whole truth*, the defense attorney asks him at what time he saw the accused leave the scene. The court expects him to answer according to the ordinary, common sense use of the word 'time' and not to conscientiously divulge his deepest belief that time does not measure the true state of affairs.

Or suppose this same friend is in a university physics seminar discussing an experiment involving the cloud-chamber tracks left by colliding high-energy particles. Now, his truest answer as to when a certain subnuclear event took place is expected to relate to the quantum mechanics level of abstraction. In this situation his response might properly include a recondite definition of "simultaneity" or even a view of time "running backwards" in the causal chain. Nevertheless, the normal participants in the courtroom and in the seminar would have little trouble keeping track of the constraints on their words.

The real difficulty comes when we humans reach out for the most comprehensive framework in which we can test an explanation. In such cases we easily risk confusing narrower assumptions associated with familiar usage with absolute meanings. This has happened over and over again throughout the history of natural science and mathematics. It also happens in music and art, as when popular spokesmen assume their present range of tastes to be the knowledgeable standard for what is proper or beautiful. Van Gogh suffered the injustice of such impermanent standards. Only one of his paintings sold during his lifetime. With Bizet it was not until after his death that his opera Carmen was well received.

'Reality'

Finally, consider how we use the word 'reality.' We say that the chair we are sitting on is real (as opposed to imaginary). If we are discussing ideas and their reality, we want at least to be clear that an idea is real at a different level of abstraction than a physical chair.

An ancient view of what is real likely included the notion of a flat earth. A flat-earth "reality" could only exist in the thoughts of men because of limitations in their view of the earth and their slight knowledge of astronomy. In order to avoid such limitation-dependent notions of reality, we will use the word 'real' to mean the state of affairs independent of its appearance from any *incomplete* viewpoint. If enlarging the scope of one's view can alter the nature of that view in a significant way, then the state of affairs indicated by the more limited view is not the real state. In this book reality is defined as the state of affairs knowable from the standpoint of the one infinite Mind.

In recent years, analytic philosophers have been mainly interested in problems connected with language and meaning. The richest field for this analysis is in the language describing human abilities. Here, the philosopher and the behavioral scientist become involved in the mind-body problem. This is the problem of determining the relationship between responses internalized as thought and those externalized as physical behavior. This will be discussed shortly under the heading of "Persons and the Mind-Body Problem."

Three Related Puzzles in Philosophy

Even the most muddled metaphysical perplexities can be resolved into meaningful questions[4] by relating them to the following three puzzles.

First Puzzle

The first puzzle is contained in the following questions: Of all the types of details that we have knowledge of, which type is fundamental to the others? Is it invisible particles, or regions of a field, or waves, or visible bodies? Or is it sensations, or emotions, or other semi-mental impressions? Or is it non-physical universals such as ideas? Or could it be that several of these types are equally basic? This puzzle is purposely as broad as can be; it surveys everything. As Professor W.V. Quine of Harvard put the basic ontological question, "What is there?"[5]

Second Puzzle

The second puzzle is an amplification of the first. It asks: How can we explain details that are quite unlike the primary type? How can we move from the elementary particulars to those at the other end of our spectrum of recognition? And, is there just one path of variation along which all the types are arranged, or are there diverging paths?

Throughout history, philosophies and religions have claimed to know the infrastructure of reality. But, generally speaking, they have never explicitly described how appearances hook up to the basic structure. Possibly the founder of Christianity had such specific details in mind when he said, "I have many things to say unto you, but ye cannot bear them now" (John 16:12). Briefly, let us consider how Plato's system fared in this respect.

Plato envisioned basic reality as an ideal realm underlying our imperfect world. He called basic reality "The Good" and said that we discern it through progressively more perfect forms of comprehension. These are ultimately the forms of such ideal things as beauty, justice, courage, wisdom, and grace, and also (somewhat incongruously) such forms as the perfect circle, triangle, etc. Also, numbers and their relationships are part of our approaching glimpse of the perfect realm. Quite different from this realm of pure, permanent *being* is our shadow-like view of it—our sensual world of appearances, always changing and *becoming*. Plato saw these crude approximations appearing as visible objects and, at an even cruder level of imitation, as imaginations and dreams.

The immediate problem with Plato's remarkable system is that geometric or spatial form appears in the mental realm that supposedly transcends space. He gave no details on how this happens except to hint that the spatial interpretation occurs as almost perfect thought looks in the opposite direction away from The Good. The general problem left unsolved by such idealistic philosophers is this: They have never furnished the specific details of a workable connection between their view of reality and our immediate perception of a physical world. Dualistic philosophers have been just as remiss. While not obliged to account for the finite in terms of the infinite or vice versa (because they believe matter and spirit to be somehow equal but separate), they have never furnished us with the mechanics of any possible interaction between the two.

Religions become dualistic when their adherents begin to rely upon faith in place of clear understanding as the sufficient link between earthly experience and an often vague reality called heaven. Here science should help religion and be an essential part of it because science is the honest effort to bridge the vagueness gap. And religion should be fundamental to science since religion motivates us to seek larger meanings and ask for more enduring criteria.

Third Puzzle

The third of our three basic puzzles asks: What is the nature of persons? This puzzle embraces the other two, so we will approach all three by briefly discussing the nature of "persons."[6]

Persons and the Mind-Body Problem

To fully explain what "persons" are requires solving what is known as the mind-body problem. Scientists can describe the chemical composition of the human body, but how should they describe the human mind and its link to the body? Is the mind as tangible as the brain at the level where reality seems to be physical? No. Is mind more tangible at some other level? Yes. 'Brain' is a poor synonym for 'mind' inasmuch as 'brain' refers to a fleshy organ under the skull whereas 'mind' signifies a family of abilities and dispositions. Most pyschologists relate mind to brain in roughly the way we relate the activity of a baseball game to a particular assemblage of bodies at a ball park.

Such a view is not without its serious problems. It is too vague. To be successful, it requires that matter-in-motion become, in baseball language, not only the commissioner, owners, managers, players, etc., but also the owning, playing, watching, and managing. This supposedly happens as matter interacts with itself through several levels of organization and abstraction. Molecules organize themselves by means of laws of random occurrence into more complex organic structures that successively reproduce evermore complex patterns of behavior, almost in violation of the physicist's law of entropy. This mounting complexity continues to gather force until somehow it achieves the ability to classify itself as being conscious and even capable of inventing the notion of "mind" and "mental event." The whole picture is one of material energy in flux. But one is compelled to ask: Why do the dispositions toward orderly distribution occur unchanged from the very "beginning" while particular physical things slowly degenerate? And precisely where is that marvelous metamorphosis that signals that mere material complexity has suddenly become consciously aware of itself?

Another way of introducing the mind-body problem is to ask: How can we relate our mentalistic descriptions of conscious behavior to our physicalistic descriptions of the same behavior? How can we relate mental events to happenings in the brain and nervous system? Ordinary talk about our thoughts, hopes, and intentions does not translate very well (not yet anyway) into talk about neurons, afferent and efferent responses, and triggering brain synapses. (Try and imagine a two-hundred line print-out from a computer representing events in one's brain as the translation of "I like music.") It translates even less into talk about electrons and protons. (Now, try to imagine a two-thousand line print-out as a translation of the sub-atomic events behind the neurological events symbolized by the two-hundred line print-out.)

This translation gap between mentalistic language and physicalistic language still remains even though philosophers like Gilbert Ryle of Oxford University have helped clear up some confusion regarding use of the term 'mind.' Professor Ryle's book *The Concept of Mind* has been in part a useful step in this direction. Ryle and others have reasonably shown that the notion of an invisible, ghostlike agency within a person's body issuing commands to his muscles and nerves is a "category-mistake." It is a type of confusion brought on by our using the two poorly understood categories (mental and physical) for characterizing a person's actions. In Ryle's view the mental and the physical are not parallel actions, nor are they interwoven. Rather, they are two descriptions of the same activity.

Behaviorism

But what is this activity? Some behavioral psychologists prefer to think of it as more adequately characterized by physicalistic descriptions. And they have been seeking to halt what they fear is the damaging effect of the category-mistake on our understanding of behavior. They are trying to find a way to translate the scientist's talk about motives, intentions, etc., back to the physical level. For a rough example, they would, where possible, eliminate the word 'desire' in the sentence "he *desired* something to eat" by translating it into something like "he *opened* the refrigerator door, *took out* bread and cheese, and *made* himself a sandwich." This translation does enhance our mental imagery, but it does not seem to eliminate the inference that intentions and goals are significantly involved in behavior. Otherwise, we might assume that the person merely had an accidently programmed succession of movements. Some reference to goal-directed activity is necessary at some level in order to describe the behavior adequately. Some scientists think such intention-descriptions can eventually be precisely correlated with neurological descriptions while others, such as philosopher D.C. Dennett of the University of California at Irving (author of *Content and Consciousness*), do not.[7]

Even if behaviorists could accomplish this translation, the question would still remain; Can physical descriptions best characterize the fundamental nature of existence?[8]

Is a Basic Description of Reality Even Possible?

There are philosophers—especially those sympathetic to the views of Hume, Wittgenstein, or the Positivists—who discourage the attempt to describe the "fundamental" nature of the universe. They believe such attempts are doomed from the start, not because they are too difficult, but because they are pseudo tasks. Two major objections are raised. The first is against the attempt to give a mentalistic description of the deepest level.

The Infinite-Regress Argument

It is claimed that for us to be able to describe the supposedly ultimate mental nature of all things— including our thought and language—we would need another level of meta-thought and metalanguage. This is to give us a standpoint outside of what we wish to think about and describe. The reason is that one cannot use a word to define itself nor a sentence to totally describe that self-same sentence. To try to do so would be like trying to grasp your right thumb with only your right thumb—or like trying to check the accuracy of a given clock by using only that clock as your standard. Going deeper, it would be like trying to measure the passage of time with that same time—or measure how much space space itself takes up. You need something other than your thumb in order to grasp your thumb; you need another kind of time against which to measure the passage of time, and so on. But then, every new meta-system you develop will require that you also be able to step outside of it in order to objectively describe it as part of the described universe. Thus, it is argued, the search for the ultimate description will either turn into an infinite regress or degenerate into an endless circularity of definitions.

This argument is an old one; but it does not work against the idealistic system we will be discussing for several reasons. First, while a thumb cannot grasp itself nor a word define itself, nevertheless, an idea does present itself. It is, in fact, the only idea that can present that precise idea. Here we make a distinction between merely *defining* or *outlining* something from the outside and actually *being* that thing. The infinite-regress argument applies to the former whereas our system will rest on the latter. We do not understand an idea from "outside" of it. Definitions and other ideas can point to it, but we understand it because we partake of it, or as Plato would say, we participate in its perfect form.

The second reason why the infinite-regress argument does not apply to our description of basic reality is largely an elaboration on the first. Mentioning it will, however, involve us for these next two paragraphs in the realm of mathematical logic. By means of logical deduction, our infinite system can be shown to be *complete* as well as *consistent*. (The outline of the proof is given in the Appendix.) By *complete* we mean capable of being completely axiomatized with initially specifiable axioms so that all truths expressible within the system are provable within the system. Saying this another way, all true statements expressible in the system can be derived as theorems from the axioms by means of the logic (rules of inference). This is no small achievement, for, ever since Kurt Gödel published his famous proof in 1931,[9] logicians have maintained that arithmetic (as well as higher mathematics rich enough to include number theory) is not complete in this sense. Furthermore, Professor Gödel presented another argument to show that any proof of the consistency of arithmetic will require assumptions from outside of arithmetic that will be as subject to doubt as the original consistency assumptions they were used to prove.

Our primitive definitions and axioms (chapter four) will present a self-contained foundation that supports all the truths ascribable to the system under its intended interpretation. Furthermore, this system contains its own interpretation. Its "individuals" are not uninterpreted symbols; they are qualities or "meanings" which do not have to be further interpreted from without. Their domain is the positive predicates or meanings basic to our thinking process and to our language. Thus, our formal system or object language contains all the elements of our metalanguage (English). To my knowledge such a system has not been previously suggested. Most logicians likely would claim that Tarski's findings on definability in formal systems show it to be impossible in other systems because of logical paradoxes that arise.

What I am claiming is that the elementary individuals in reality are meanings, predicates, or attribuates of a single mindlike substance rather than being separate, finite elements. This infinite system displays a formal structure because it contains all those attributes usually associated with structure—such as support, order, connectedness, directness, and stability. It also contains all the other positive meanings discernable in human experience. This will become clearer once the syntax and semantics of this new theory of meaning have been presented.

With a universal Mind, there is no need to get outside of Mind in order to recognize its attributes. Mind itself is doing the ultimate recognizing. Given, by hypothesis, that the attributes of Mind are the very elements of awareness by which we experience and understand anything, it will follow that we must experience these meanings from within the system. Indeed, the only other standpoint from which to interpret such an infinite system is to hypothesize a limited, mortal standpoint. The finite or mortal view will be discussed in chapters five and six.

So far, in examining why some philosophers and scientists feel that a basic description of reality is not possible, we have discussed their infinite-regress argument against mentalistic descriptions. Now we look at an argument raised against physicalistic descriptions. The argument is based upon the uncertainty principle set forth in 1927 by a young theoretical physicist, Werner Hiesenberg.

The Uncertainty Principle

On first examination, the mathematics of the uncertainty principle[10] implies that the details of subatomic reality are more delicate than our processes of observation. In trying to observe these delicate details we inevitably alter them. The ray of light—even the single photon of light—used in detecting the position and energy state of an elementary particle, must hopelessly change either the position or the energy associated with that particle. Thus, it is claimed, we can never know the intimate details of reality as they occur in their unobserved state. Our knowing is itself a physical process that participates in the physical scene and alters it before it can be fully described.

Neils Bohr, in his Copenhagen interpretation of quantum physics, emphasized that the problem is one of deciding where the dividing line is between observer and observation.

But all these arguments beg the fundamental question by assuming that the elementary events and the process of knowing about them are already known to be physical. They further assume a theory of truth that is itself questionable. This is the correspondence theory of truth which holds that truth is an abstract relationship that comes into being only when we correlate language symbols and their meanings with an otherwise meaningless reality. Chapter four will present our theory of truth, which, simply stated, is that truth is one of the inherent meanings of a system of meanings that are all the attributes of a single substance called Mind.

The deeper implication to be drawn from the indeterminacy principle is not that the limits of knowledge are the consequences of an inevitable crudeness in our physical observations. Rather, the limits of human knowledge arise in our trying to apply finite concepts to a non-finite reality. Finite concepts depict reality in the classical terms of material points (Newton's influence on the concept of reality) and continuous but finite fields (Maxwell's influence). If we press these concepts to their limit in quantum physics, the contradictory result is the appearance of a discontinuous reality describable only in terms of probabilities—the probabilities of its appearance under this or that description.

Our traditional concepts of position, distance, direction, the change of these in respect to time, and of an instant in time are all faulty. At best they are incomplete views of Mind and its infinite system. Even relativity theory shows that such parameters vary according to the observer's frame of reference so that only their combination is invariant. The Copenhagen interpretation of the complementarity principle of quantum physics holds that even their combination cannot yield a completely sound description. For, while the concepts of position and momentum (or particle and wave) are almost complementary, they overlap sufficiently so that if we completely hold to either one we violate the integrity of the other.[11] Using finite concepts to describe reality is like trying to map the spherical earth onto a flat surface; distortion is built into the mapping because flatness has insufficient dimensions to represent a sphere.

The major effort in the last seventy years toward a more complete description of reality has been in the sciences. But not without a curious twist. Physicists have been seeing matter and energy as more of a mathematical, conceptual structure; whereas analytic philosophers have been more and more regarding mind as the name we use to characterize a select set of physical events. These philosophers tend to leave ontology (the science of being and its necessary constituents and relations) to the physicist and epistemology (the theory of how we have knowledge) to the researcher who is examining the brain and its cybernetic model in a computer. Nevertheless, these converging paths indicate continuing movement toward a unified theory encompassing the present separate levels of description.

3 Touching Relativity and Quantum Physics

Quantum Physics

The difficulty with the uncertainty principle previously mentioned brings us to the kind of problem that scientists are presently facing in quantum physics. Using huge, high-energy particle accelerators, physicists have been breaking down the sub-atomic particles into even more basic particles in their search for the ultimate essence of matter and its alter-ego, physical energy. This research is in a very unsettled, if not chaotic state for want of a theory that can successfully tie together all the anomalies being uncovered. So far, scientists have not been able to put together a theoretical model that can successfully explain all the strange things that happen in their high-energy experiments. Even the mathematical manipulation of the equations describing the experiments produces undesirable "infinities" which keep ballooning their way into the results (The denominators of certain important ratios tend toward zero, and thus the ratios tend toward infinity.) The mathematician-physicist at present has to arbitrarily subtract out these infinities by using a process called renormalization in order to make the results agree with his observations.[1]

In general, physicists presently accept a theory of matter that describes the dynamics of its sub-atomic particles in terms of probability functions rather than in terms of definite position and definite momentum for any given instant. This amounts to treating them as waves. The probability-description yields a prediction of what will occur in some types of experiments even though it seems conceptually unsatisfying. It seems unsatisfying partly because people want to retain their comfortable habit of thinking of the real world as constructed out of things occupying definite space and having duration in definite time. Carried to its limit, this would yield a world constructed out of things analyzable into smaller and smaller volumes approaching dimensionless points. These infinitesmal points must still be qualitatively variable; they must be disposed to manifest different forms of energy or to react differently at different times. They must if they are to cause our perception of a world of varying color, temperature, elasticity, etc. But right here is where quantum theory and its uncertainty principle contradict any such attempt to pinpoint existence.

The debate continues among philosopher-physicists: Is it the interaction of our relatively crude tools of perception with the particles that brings on the uncertainty relationship? Is it the incompleteness of our constructs called "particle" and "wave" that makes each inadequate for particularizing the actual state of affairs? Is it the "psychic attempt" on the part of the observer to conceive of a kind of knowledge that is true only for an instant (instantaneous position and momentum) that is self-defeating? Is it our inability to separate the observer from the observation at the basic level that contradicts our conceptual mold? In any event the physicist has not found a fully satisfying answer. His quest within a finite frame is suggestive of trying to reach "the carrot at the end of the stick." Each step toward a satisfactory finite explanation keeps pushing that alluring explanation always one step beyond reach.

General Relativity alias Spacetime "Geometrodynamics"

Turning from quantum "infinitesmals" to research by way of the immense, we find new views on space and time. Theoretical physicists, working with Einstein's general relativity equations have extended these equations over the past twenty years into a body of theory called spacetime physics or geometrodynamics.

In Einstein's latter years there was a falling away of professional interest in general relativity; increasingly Einstein stood alone in his convictions. He wrote to a cousin on March 30, 1950: "After years and years of incessant effort I perfected the theory of relativity, but because of the enormous mathematical difficulties am unable to judge whether the completion of the theory hit the mark correctly. The present generation of my colleagues think not."[2] (Another reason for his isolation was his strong conviction that in quantum physics the so-called uncertainty principle was not a complete principle of nature. He saw it as an ad hoc statistical law enabling physicists to make-do until they could find the complete representation.)[3]

Since 1955 there has been vigorously renewed interest

in general relativity. This has been partly due to new observational data in favor of GR and partly due to the extension of GR into the more dynamic mathematical model called geometrodynamics or GMD. The attractiveness of the GMD model of the universe is that it is close to achieving the status of the full unified field theory that Einstein devoted the last half of his life to finding. (Simply put, the unified field theory seeks to account for all physical phenomena by means of a single and consistent mathematical model. This mathematical model has generally been interpreted as mirroring the complexities of the gravitation field.)

The mathematical formulations in such an assessment are formidable. According to John C. Graves of the Massachusetts Institute of Technology, in his book *Conceptual Foundations of Contemporary Relativity Theory* (M.I.T. Press, 1971), a number of scientists believe that GMD has hit the mark in unifying the explanation of the gravitational and the electromagnetic fields. They now feel that only the gap with quantum physics remains to be closed. John Archibald Wheeler of Princeton University, the foremost physicist in the extension of general relativity, has stated his belief that GMD has the dynamic richness to accomplish this task. GMD already provides the best explanation to date for the new discoveries concerning pulsars and the collapse of giant stars into supernova and possible black holes.

GMD postulates that matter and its associated phenomena can be described in terms of modifications occurring in the geometry of space. In fact, up until about 1965, the GMD theorists believed that everything in the physical universe could be totally accounted for in terms of nothing more than the complex curvature of "empty" spacetime. A half century earlier, Einstein had reasonably shown how both gravitation and acceleration were manifestations of the curvature[4] of spacetime. Geometro-dynamic theory carries this radical program further by claiming that matter itself is composed of particular modes of intense curvature and disturbance. This was a new Copernican revolution. Prior to this, the gravitational and electromagnetic fields were viewed as emanating *from* matter, whereas now it was being claimed that matter is the manifestation of the spacetime geometry. Instead of graviation causing spacetime to warp, gravitation itself was now viewed as warped spacetime geometry. In Dr. Wheeler's own earlier words (in a paper delivered at a symposium in 1960 on the role of mathematics in the formulation of physical theories):

> Is the physical world in which we live a purely mathematical construct? Put the question in another way: Is spacetime only an arena within which fields and particles move about as "physical" and "foreign" entities? Or is the four-dimensional continuum all there is? Is curved empty geometry a kind of magic building material out of which everything in the physical world is made: (1) slow curvature in one region of space describes a gravitation field; (2) a rippled geometry with a different type of curvature somewhere else describes an electromagnetic field; (3) a knotted-up region of high curvature describes a concentration of charge and mass-energy that moves like a particle? Are fields and particles foreign entities immersed in geometry, or are they nothing but geometry?

> It would be difficult to name any issue more central to the plan of physics than this: whether spacetime is only an arena, or whether it is everything. [John A. Wheeler, "Curved Empty Spacetime as the Building Material of the Physical World: An Assessment," *Logic, Methodology, and Philosophy of Science*, eds. Nagel, Suppes, and Tarski. (Stanford, Calif.: Stanford Univ. Press, 1962) Quoted with permission.]

It remained to be seen whether spacetime in its mathematical clothing had sufficient attributes to be

able to account for its own self-actuation and transforma-
tion. Apparently it did not, and by the mid 1960's Dr.
Wheeler and some of his colleagues were voicing a different view. This was that, while spacetime appears to be
the basic clay from which the physical universe is
fashioned, it is only a thin slice of a "superspace" that
includes all possible arrangements of the spacetime field.
Furthermore, neither spacetime nor superspace appear to
be the ultimate causative force that fashions the
spacetime clay. This causative substance was now tentatively suggested as some kind of dimensionless "pre-
geometry" undergirding spacetime. Several years later,
the new view was made a little clearer. In the 1279 page
graduate-level physics textbook *Gravitation* by Misner,
Thorne and Wheeler (W.H. Freeman and Co., 1973) the
authors (particularly Dr. Wheeler) speculate in the final
pages on what the mysterious pregeometry might be like.
What is the nature of something that is logically prior to
time and space? Their tentative suggestion is that it may
be a generator of logical relationships—a self-generating
"calculus of propositions" that has the compelling
simplicity of the two-value logic (yes/no, true/false, or
present/absent).

While these authors do not go so far as to say so, yet
what could sound more like a description of a mental
system than such speculations on a self-actuating calculus of propositions that is dimensionless in the spatio-
temporal sense? The terminology "calculus of propositions" suggests the calculus of ideas developed in this
present book. Something else the authors of *Gravitation*
discuss is equally germane to the theory presented here.
It is the claim that "empty space" is not empty but is
instead the seat of the most violent physics—the constant
collapse and rebirth of the gravitational field. They de-

scribe it as a "virtual foam-like structure" of positive and negative fluctuations where the basic particles are created and annihilated. We will refer to this foam-like structure in more detail in chapter six.

Implications of the New Physics

It is philosophically significant that GMD theorists have posited a single substance, the gravitation-field geometry to account for all physical phenomena. This is an attempt to get beneath the age-old duality of the container versus the contained, the "framework-ness" of spacetime versus the "thing-ness" of the material point, or the continuum versus the discrete. The search for this ultimate single essence rested for a while on the dynamic geometry of spacetime. But now some physicists are thinking of a pregeometry that is dimensionless but not attributeless.

Of equal philosophical significance, this ultimate substance seems to be more and more recognizable as having characteristics that are mindlike rather than physical.[5] Witness it described as geometry, logic, akin to a calculus of propositions, axiomlike, and logically prior to spacetime.

Probing Beneath the Spacetime Assumption

Almost two hundred years ago, Immanuel Kant, 57 years of age and a relatively obscure professor of logic and metaphysics at the University of Köningsberg in East Prussia, presented to the world his monumental work, the *Critique of Pure Reason*. In this prodigious book, he claimed that space and time were forms of perception and that the human mind was so constructed that it necessarily imposed these forms on its primitive data in order for it to have any tangible intuitions at all. Because the intellect necessarily deals in these forms of space and time, pure reason can never probe successfully beneath this self-created boundary. Therefore, *pure reason* is sorely limited in its ability to do useful metaphysics. (Kant claimed, though, that moral action and *practical reason* can go beyond the confines of phenomena and apprehend the moral law of God.) While I differ fundamentally with Kant on his definitions of "pure reason" and "practical reason," yet we will come close to one of Kant's views regarding space and time. Kant saw space and time as the *necessary* forms of "intuition." We shall see them as necessary only for distinguishing the details of experience *quantitatively*, that is, by means of finite beginnings and endings. But when we distinguish the details of experience in their full light, we perceive a deeper, larger, *qualitative* individuality.

By habit, we think of space as *quantitative*, and we customarily use this "quantitativeness" as the basis for trying to visualize what the words 'infinite' and 'infinitesmal' mean. Likewise, we use our quantitative notion of time to try to picture an "instant" and an "eternity." We picture the instant as occurring *within time* and eternity as made up *of time*. But this procedure will prove inadequate for our purposes here.

Our infinite system differs from a vast collection of finite spaces or moments. It is not even the accretion of *infinitely many* finite parts.[6] Nor is it "built up" in the way that the intuitionist in mathematical theory conceives of mathematical truths as being built up from recursive functions. Instead, it is to be understood as one whole substance with a denumerable* domain of primary attributes. Each one of these attributes is omnipresent or everywhere available.

But what does this mean? In what other ways would such an infinite system differ from a finite one? How does it relate to present mathematical concepts of infinity? How can it be tangible or have concrete meaning to us? And what kind of language would describe it? The rest of this chapter offers some preliminary exercises expanding our view in preparation for the journey that will answer these questions.

What is the Ultimate Framework?

At first glance, space and time seem to frame everything we experience (except of course, spacetime itself). But do these parameters frame thought? Obviously, our thoughts, glimmers of understanding, and principles—as well as prejudices and fears—are of one or more levels of abstraction differing from the level of objects defined in spacetime. The "thinkability" of an idea does not depend upon our being at any particular place.

Someone could object. He could argue that our entertainment of ideas seems to be independent of space only because we carry our brain's memory banks with us wherever we are. Furthermore, he might point out that brain states are themselves arrangements of cells, paths, and electrical charges in space. This is a reasonable objection.[7] But it will not prevail if we are able to show how bodies, cells, and electrical charges can be resolved

---

*"Denumerable" in mathematics refers to the lowest order of infinity, the order that corresponds to the infinite series of whole numbers.

into mental constructs similar to the set-theoretic* constructs of mathematics and then show how these mental constructs stem from incomplete views of an even more basic property-theoretic or quality-theoretic system.

"Self-Evident Feelings" and Mathematicians

The difficulty in assaying our feeling that space is an objective reality is that we are so accustomed to this feeling we accept it at face value. This tendency is rooted deeper in our thought than any early tendency of men to believe that the sun daily circles the earth. Consider the space housing your body. This space seems such an inescapable aspect of existence that it seems self-evident that fundamental existence cannot be divorced from space. But is it absolutely true? Over the past one-hundred years, mathematicians have learned to discount such self-evident feelings arising from physical observation.

Prior to about 1850 most mathematicians believed it a self-evident absolute truth that through any two points just one straight line can be drawn.[8] They now realize that this is not an absolute truth but only a useful rule to adopt if we decide to restrict ourselves to our familiar (and possibly simplistic) mode of thinking. Such a rule is similar to one about parallel lines adopted by Euclid when he formulated what we now call Euclidean geometry. Mathematicians no longer claim that such rules apply to the universe as seen from the broadest possible perspective or from the requirements of any ultimate law of logic. Our sense of Euclidean space—flat space as the physicists call it—seems true enough within our familiar world embracing our mode of viewing,

---

*"Set theoretic means that sets (including the empty set) are the fundamental individuals of the theory or system.

measuring, moving about, etc. Its relative truth, though, depends upon how one defines a straight line—as the shortest distance between objects, the line of most-parallel transport, the path that light travels between events, etc.

Einstein held that one of the non-Euclidean geometries was better suited for describing the laws of the physical universe. Subsequent observations of astronomers have tended to confirm his theory that the shortest paths across the universe lie on curves—also that between any two points at least two straight lines can be drawn. (This can be roughly visualized if we imagine space as somehow similar to the surface of a sphere. Then, between any two points in this space, there is a path around one side of the sphere and another path around the other side. And if the points are at opposite poles then there is an infinite number of pairs of straight lines between them.)

Generally speaking, we have not yet learned to be as careful as mathematicians in respect to what we consider absolutely true. It probably appears absolutely true that the place where you now are extends from your immediate location over to the nearby wall or surroundings. And it likely appears absolutely true that your own physicality is embodied out of this same kind of extendedness. Your head, limbs, torso, feet, and fingers all have their sizes, boundaries, beginnings, and endings structured in and of space. Furthermore, it seems that, at any one instant, this space-structure is independent of consciousness, yours, mine, or anyone's. Space seems actually to be out there all around us while consciousness seems to be located nowhere: only metaphorically is it called "inner space." And since whatever you or I think during the next few seconds is not likely to make the walls and furniture fly outward or draw closer, it seems safe to conclude that consciousness does not directly affect space. But before we conclude that space is primordial to consciousness or that consciousness can take place only within physical space, we ought to learn more about consciousness and its healthy, affirmative operation.

Consciousness

Indicative of humanity's lack of understanding in this area is the tendency for psychologists to be able to explain the abnormal operations of the mental mechanism with more conviction than its healthy aspects. Try to find in the professional literature an explanation of intelligence, love, or honesty. Surprisingly little information is ventured on these topics in psychology textbooks, and yet a great deal can be found on schizophrenic reactions, aggression, and amnesia. Popularized books and articles are focusing on how to realize more love, confidence, openness; but these writings generally do not pretend to explain, in a way acceptable to other scientists, what love actually is, or courage, or honesty. Sometimes the operational definitions given in serious textbooks are hardly more positive than the somewhat humorous definition of a good consciousness as a healthy fear of getting caught—or the youngster's definition of memory as "the thing I forget with." Nevertheless, psychologists are developing some useful techniques and a vast body of observational data with which to work. It is the need for a general theory to undergird psychology that is so urgent.

We ask again: Is existence in spacetime basically independent of consciousness or of anything remotely similar to what we think of as consciousness? Lay aside the weaker claim that our present geographical location is the result, in part, of our past desires and motivations. (The materialist can argue that such desires are themselves subject to the prior existence of space and time).

Before anyone answers our question on the basis that it is "self-evident" that space and time actually exist independent of consciousness, let him consider a type of temporary, "self-evident certainty" we frequently have. This is the knowledge of space and time we encounter in our night dreams. In our dreams our dream selfhood sees itself in a spatio-temporal world which is every bit as real as itself. This dream world has its distances, motions, and durations—woozy and muddled but nevertheless as substantial as our dream selfhood. But when we awake—experience a refocusing of consciousness—the seeming objective existence of this space and time vanishes. We see at once that it was only the construction of certain poorly understood operations in our thinking process.

It is significant that entirely within a dream there exists both objectivity and subjectivity. If you are dreaming of a hard-fought tennis match, the tennis court and the participants all have objective existence within the dream while the hopes you experience about the progress of the match have subjective existence. Of course, whatever is objective from within your dream still turns out to be subjective to your awakened view.

The analogy with dreams is simplistic and thus of little use beyond suggesting that the objectivity we ascribe to our spacetime world might turn out to be yet another equally subjective construction. We will need a better line of attack if we are to understand in detail how the "here" and the "there" of spacetime can be a mental ordering. The Bible implies it is mental. Luke reports the Pharisees asking Jesus when the kingdom of God should come. He reportedly answered, "The kingdom of God cometh not with observation: Neither shall they say, Lo here! or, Lo there! for, the kingdom of God is within you."*

For one more illustration of how the unthinking acceptance of our familiar sense of space influences us, consider how we commonly view the process of knowing about something. If asked whether we can know about something while it is at a distance from us, we might answer, "Yes; knowing is different than holding or touching." But in giving such an answer, notice how we have immediately focused on the "knowing" instead of challenging the concept of "external distance." We generally believe that when someone knows about a distant event, he has internal thoughts that represent the external event. Or we believe that he has something physical happening in his brain that is related to the distant event by means of a chain of physical reactions. Either explanation is designed to eliminate any slightest hint that "to know" is to use a mysterious mental "force" that reaches out through space like a radar signal. But we can also stay clear of this improbable notion that thoughts travel through space by modifying our notion of space.[9]

In the next chapter I shall develop the hypothesis that existence rests upon an infinite system called Mind. In developing the details of the hypothesis, my immediate aim is not to convince the reader of their credibility; the immediate aim is to determine what is required to achieve internal consistency. As in mathematics, these requirements will appear quite abstract because they are at a different level of abstraction than our physical experiences.

The next task after determining the requirements and formulating a set of axioms, is to see if the system is believable. We do this, starting in chapter five, by at-

---

*However, some modern translators render the Greek of Luke 17:21 as "the kingdom of God is now among you" or "in your midst."

tempting an informal deduction from the axioms. Hopefully, this deductive argument arrives at our familiar view—accounting for the way our type of thinking perceives a finite universe. To convince the reader, this part of the theory needs to be valid.

If the informal argument opens the way for some readers to agree that the conclusions follow from the hypothesis, then eventually the starting hypothesis will need to be put to an empirical test. An idea of how such a test might be designed is given in chapter seven.

4 The Infinite System

Four Apparent Requirements for the Hypothesis

We explain why objects fall by applying the principle of gravity to specific cases. One gravitational principle binds together an infinity of possible cases.* We do not have to look for a separate principle of gravity for bricks and another for dry leaves—nor one principle for the earth and an entirely separate principle for the moon where things weigh less. Explanations tend toward a single, multifaceted principle with infinitely many potential applications. As Einstein once said, "We are seeking for the simplest possible system of thought which will

---

*Nominalists who try to avoid talking about principles as if they were make-believe entities, may view the principle in a physical way—as a field. Then, even though there are roughly as many local gravitational fields as there are distinct bodies, each local field is still part of the one continuous, universal gravitational field. Each local system is like a small wrinkle or whirlpool of curvature within the big quivering pudding called spacetime.

bind together the observed facts."

Just as we usually expect a common principle to link similar events, so, if we go deep enough, we expect to find a law-like relationship linking dissimilar events. They are also happening in the same universe. But at times we have to drastically revise our concept of the universe in order to see these relationships. Regardless of the cost in enlarging our viewpoint, there still remains that deep feeling that beneath every mystery there is an intelligible explanation. Our world can be subdivided and compartmentalized, but the compartments are still linked within the whole. If we can understand why water boils by accepting a theory about molecules, we are not likely to be satisfied with an explanation of why water freezes that makes no mention of molecules. We do not honestly believe that phenomena can exist in totally unrelated isolation.

Most of us are attracted to the idea that there is not only an underlying principle embracing physical descriptions of life, but that the ultimate explanation also accounts for our mentalistic descriptions as well. Chapters two and three already suggested why finite systems are inherently unable to provide such a comprehensive principle. If we tentatively agree, then it is not unreasonable to explore how the idea of *one Mind* might serve as the underlying principle. The main pitfall to be avoided in exploring what, up to now, has largely been a religious view, is to avoid skipping blithely from one level of abstraction to another without accounting for the steps in between. We overlook these specific steps only on pain of becoming scientifically unintelligible.

Structural Requirements

What are the requirements for such a one-Mind system? Doubtless, its attributes must be non-physical, for otherwise it would not be mindlike in any obvious manner. In other words, we will not want to describe Mind as heavy, tall, or pale blue. Though sooner or later we will have to account for the role such terms play in the overall scheme of things.

To avoid a very sticky problem, the attributes must remain the qualities of *one single substance* instead of becoming separate substances themselves. For as soon as we hypothesize totally separate substances at the primary level, we no longer have a basis for relating them to each other—without going to still another more basic level (which would violate our assumption that we are already talking about the basic level). Totally separate substances would be unrelatable; and this would beget pluralism and mysticism which is contrary to our theory's original aim.

Furthermore, if all primary distinctions arise from separate substances, then it is unlikely that attributes can also account for distinctions. Attributes could be brought into the picture only as abstractions from a collection of primary substances. And we could no longer call our universe a one-Mind system. Instead, it would be more appropriate to think of it as a giant brainlike system. If we dissect a brain, we find no thoughts or meanings embedded within its fleshy cells. Analyzing further, we eventually come to molecules, atoms, and electrons. Since none of these things can think (otherwise, by hypothesis, they themselves would be brains) we cannot have thoughts or ideas constituting a brain's primary level. Nor could we at the universe's primary level if we adopt a multiple-substance theory. Fundamental reality would be merely a vast collection of separate "atoms," while thought and language would be abstractions arising from their meaningless animation.

However, if only one substance occurs at the primary level, then its different attributes must generate all the individuality and variety within the universe. Such a single, unitary substance would provide the basis for relating any attribute to any other. If this substance is mindlike, then we should be able to say that its intelligence is related not only to its substance but also to its freedom, joy, and beauty. We need to be able to see the relationships between any of its qualities as a relationship where each describes an aspect of the others. Then it will follow that every possible connection between individual attributes exists. Beauty must express intelligence, and freedom must include discipline and joy.

We could refer to the one substance by any of its attributes. Humanity already uses a host of expressive names—the Almighty, Father, Providence, Love, Spirit, The Great Spirit, Father-Mother God, the Father of lights, Truth, and so on in every culture and language.

In accord with the preceding ideas, we will require of our hypothesis the following:

1. Our infinite system is to be based on one and only one substance. This substance must be mindlike and have denumerably many primary attributes. Each of these will, in a sense, be descriptive of each of the others because each is descriptive of the one substance underlying them all.
2. Our infinite system is to involve only one cause. This follows from the above requirement. It also is necessary to avoid an endless circularity of causes for each event in the universe.
3. The one cause must have infinitely many effects. Otherwise we will need more than one cause to account for the infinite diversity of life.
4. Our infinite system must account for the difference between a generic class and the members of that class. Materialistic systems generally view the in-

dividual tree, the particular animal, or the specific
rock as the primary reality while treating the
generic class—oak, man, or basalt—as a generali-
zation one step removed from actual existence.
This assumes that existence is founded in space and
time—an assumption that looks all the more shaky
as we examine the requirements for a viable foundation for existence.

Filling The Structure

In arriving at the foregoing structure, I have drawn upon
the ideas of many scientists and philosophers. The ideas
to fill these structural requirements, however, have come
mainly from Judeo-Christian monotheism. The theme I
have followed is the thread running through the Old and
New Testaments that true wealth or substance is
spiritual and not subject to rust or decay. The Bible does
not ignore material well-being or "signs following," but
it stresses that material evidence is the surface indicator
rather than the actual substance. Few religions go so far
as to interpret Jesus' statement, "It is the spirit that
quickeneth; the flesh profiteth nothing" as implying matter is a misrepresentation of the substance that quickens
our lives, yet this is the interpretation I find convincing.

The axiomatic approach we will use in presenting the
infinite system was suggested in part by the way the 17th
century philosopher Spinoza axiomatized his hypothesis
of an infinite substance. Spinoza was not the first Western philosopher to think that the universe was the manifestation of one substance. Apart from a long line of
Hebrew prophets who hewed to this monolithic ideal,
several early Greek philosophers tried to develop an ontology based upon one substance.[1]

Spinoza's Bold Approach

Spinoza claimed the unity of reality and the consequent unreality of finite things.[2] He defined substance as that which cannot be related to anything outside of itself. And he called this one substance God. Even so, from two prominent quarters, Spinoza was accused of being an atheist because of his unorthodoxy. Later, he was called a pantheist because his God seemed too closely related to the physical universe. This was partly because Spinoza held that, while God had infinitely many attributes, only two of these attributes were knowable to man—these two being "thought" and "extension in space." Our premise is different since it holds that spatial extension is finite and cannot be an attribute of infinite Mind. Furthermore, we claim that each attribute of Mind is necessarily knowable. This is because we posit the attributes of Mind as the very essence of knowing and knowability.

Spinoza started with a number of axioms describing substance. From these and a series of deductions, he sought to arrive at our familiar view of the world. This procedure of starting with assumptions about the cosmic totality obviously has its difficulties, and it has been out of favor with pragmatic philosophers for years. As scientific discoveries about nature, mathematics, and logic began to multiply at the turn of this century, philosophy professors became uncomfortably aware of the blunders embedded in their earlier speculations; a cautious outlook set in. Philosophers began to demand more honest rigour of themselves and their methodology than had the earlier system builders. Happily, this attitude has helped disperse many lofty fogbanks of academic erudition.

The present cautious mood does not mean, however, that the all-embracing hypothesis is permanently out of favor. The long-run tendency demands balance between immediate, tangible results and understandable, comprehensive theory. Science operates by both inductive and deductive reasoning. Its genius is to rise from immediate experience and step imaginatively beyond the known to find systems of thought that bind together our most accurate observations. But in the short run, induction and deduction are not usually in exact balance. A season of technological advancement—producing its better microscopes and telescopes—brings a harvest of new evidence. This must be evaluated in the light of the available theoretical structure. If serious questions remain or new riddles come to light, then inquiring minds will soon be reaching for new and better hypotheses that can be sown in the proving ground of reason and their deductive fruits again tested against experience.

Through these stages of planting and harvesting, along with advances in mathematics and logic, men and women are continually in a better position to make the inductive leap from the immediately observable to better hypotheses about reality and its infrastructure. Whenever a new theory better fits the phenomena we observe, it may become the new paradigm or model upon which scientists base their reasoning. Thus, we leave behind a stationary, flat earth for a spinning, orbiting planet; Ptolemaic heavens for Copernican heliocentricity; and thus we now fit Newtonian laws into the larger framework of Einstein. Thomas Kuhn says in his book, *The Structure of Scientific Revolutions* that such new paradigms are the basis for scientific revolutions in the history of human thought.

Spinoza's method is an ambitious attempt to employ the scientist's hypothetico-deductive approach at the deepest level. Used here, it allows us to introduce the radical hypothesis that spacetime is not external to consciousness but is instead the construct of a limited viewpoint. This bold leap enables us to examine this hypothesis directly rather than inch our way in this direction—pushed by the trend of new ideas and discoveries. Of late, the observations of more and more scientists are hinting to a greater unity of mind and body and between every part of the universe from the smallest mitochondria multiplying within our cells to the farthest reaches of galactic space.[3]

Key Source of Ideas

As mentioned, the content to fill our tentative framework has been drawn mainly from the religious view that spiritual substance actually exists and that it alone supports all valid experience. This view has been advanced in varying degrees by religions throughout history. Scriptures held sacred by Eastern religions have developed aspects of this theme in their own way. In ancient India some teachers taught that the sensual world was a web of illusions. The Western world's Old and New Testaments abound with references implying that beneath the vicissitudes of mortal experience there is an everpresent spiritual bedrock that is unshakable.

Apparently, the most unequivocal statement of the view that reality is entirely spiritual and infinite and that finite forms are therefore illusory mental impressions is that set forth by the New England author and religious leader Mary Baker Eddy. She first circulated this view more than a hundred years ago, and for thirty-five years she clarified and enlarged on these ideas by writing and revising her book *Science and Health with Key to the Scriptures*. I have leaned heavily on *Science and Health* and have borrowed countless ideas from it in developing the hypothesis for this theory, although the casual reader will be hard pressed to find the specific instances. I do not claim to have plumbed the full depth of Mrs. Eddy's book or the full depth of the Bible. The interested reader should test these two books firsthand.

The first chapter of Genesis in the Bible served in a slight way as a suggestive guide for the seven axioms which follow.

Finally—lest some readers be disappointed that the axioms are cast in informal philosophical language rather than purely formalized structure—it should be noted that at this stage of development this theory is of necessity a work of philosophy rather than a specific science. Many formal structures, however, are embedded in the axioms, and part of one of these structures (a new foundation for set theory) has been abstracted from axioms IV through VII and used in the Appendix.

The Infinite System Axioms

I—One Substance   There is one Mind. Mind is the one and only substance. This is to say that Mind is self-existent and eternal and dependent upon nothing outside of its own infinitude.

II—Basic Action   Mind is self-revealing. It emits well-focused ideas to itself by reflecting upon its own nature. This reflection or self-awareness illuminates its own harmonious action.

III—Overall Effect   Creation is the intelligible, continuously unfolding effect within the one Cause, Mind. This effect is continuous and well-ordered, although it is not temporal. It is the simultaneous object of Mind's understanding. Creation is spiritual or incorporeal—which means it is not in a form that is individuated by finite beginnings and endings. Its variety is individualized by means of qualities which are the attributes and ideas of Mind.

IV—Prime Attributes   The elementary attributes that distinguish creation can be considered to be "primes" or primary qualities. These are not further analyzable except in terms of the one substance—just as prime numbers are not further divisible other than by themselves and the number one.

Each prime quality is unique; and because of this, it is incomparable in the sense that it is neither more nor less, better nor worse than any other prime quality. There is no hierarchy of values among the primes. There is, however, an orderly relationship among them that locates each one in Mind. They can be ordered according to their degree of similarity somewhat in the way that colors of the light spectrum can be serially arranged in an artist's color wheel.

Each quality is a hue of spiritual light that enhances each of the others. Their interaction includes no inharmony because they are already harmoniously united as attributes of the same substance. In human affairs, fashion often dictates which colors, shapes, and patterns go well together—until a new fashion comes into vogue. In nature, ecological systems evolve to a delicate balance that can be jarred by sudden intrusion or clash. Whereas at the deeper level of spiritual reality, the combinations of Mind's attributes are always beautifully self-reinforcing. They supercede time and so are ever fresh and original.

Our human view of these elements of awareness appears as the meanings we associate with the nouns, verbs, and adjectives that predicate perfection to various aspects of life. A few of these meanings are *accuracy, balance, joy, strength, harmony, purity, vitality, freedom, abundance, love, clarity, grace, intelligence, peace, receptivity, health, understanding, constancy, flexibility, protection, continuity,* and *wisdom*.

Such positive meanings represent the undefined primitives in both the ontology and the epistemology of this system. They are both the elementary building blocks of reality and the basic elements of knowledge. Knowing and being are united at the deepest level.

Since each quality describes Mind, each can be considered descriptive of its complementary qualities taken collectively. And, to a lesser extent, each is descriptive of each of the others taken individually. For example, the quality called "truth" tells us that all the other qualities taken together necessarily express truth. It also tells us that each of the others, such as beauty, is true—a true attribute of Mind. In return, beauty tells us that what is really true must be beautiful. (We will see later that because a human view is at best an incomplete view, it is not completely true. Therefore the human scene is not totally beautiful. Conversely, the mortal sense of beauty is not completely true.)

V—Compound Attributes

Mind also manifests its intelligence by combining primes into compound ideas. Think of musical notes being composed into musical phrases, then into passages, and movements, and finally into a fully orchestrated symphony. In like manner, Mind composes its ideas—giving each composition an individuality beyond that of its component primes and compounds. Yet each compound is always factorable into distinct primes. Thus, the primes are fulfilling infinitely many roles simultaneously in expressing their individuality and in participating in the hierarchy of compound ideas. The individual notes in Mind's symphony never lose their own distinct identity. Appreciation is the ability to detect the individual identities within a compound idea. And appreciation is itself a detectable attribute.

While all the primes are of equal importance and value, the compounds form hierarchies of value according to their ascending magnitude or scope. Consider the idea "cattle" in the first chapter of Genesis. This idea includes more components than do the ideas "herb" or "grass." A compound of one hundred primes is of higher rank than a compound of, say, thirty primes. And yet, there is not the slightest disparagement imputed to a lower ranking; the lesser compound is as necessary as the greater if there is to be the greater embracing it. A man does not feel smugly superior to his own arm even though he has some dominion over this member of his body. Nor should he be patronizing or demeaning toward any other less-compound expression of Mind such as the simple beast—nor toward other men who, in the human view of fortune's circumstances, presently see less of their own wholeness.

Without any one expression there would be less enhancement of the others. Without the idea of "child" the more compound idea "adult" would be incomplete. Without the wheel, the wagon* would be lacking; and without "wagon" there would be less use for "wheel." Because each positive idea is unique, no other idea can ever supplant it in the divine order. How could courage diminish the peculiar worth of grace? How could wisdom impair strength by their union—or weaken justice?

---

*"Wheel" and "wagon" are not purely spiritual concepts since they include a spatio-temporal connotation. They are used here for their convenient analogy.

VI—Identities   Mind unfolds still another dimension of being as it reflects upon its creative nature. This is the multiplication of each of the primes and most of the compounds into uniquely individualized views or interpretations. Each individual view is identified with its archtype idea. We will call each view an identity of that idea, even though it has its own individuality. An idea represents the archtype or generic class (intension) of infinitely many (denumerably many) views (extensions) of itself. We can use mathematical terminology and say that Mind is the one-many *relation* that maps each idea *onto* its many identities. Conversely, Mind also is the *function* that reflects the identities back *into* their respective generic ideas. For example, the generic, compound idea man is multiplied as individual men and women. And men and women, seen spiritually, are individualized identities of the generic idea man.

The individuality of each identity comes from the peculiar way it is related to its context. Consider a prime idea. If we compare a particular prime to an individual flower, then each of its identities is like a slightly different photograph of that flower. Each photograph has its own individuality because it reveals a slightly different angle or lighting or background. Thus each photo in each generic class is unique even though every photo in that class represents the same flower.

In the case of a compound idea, the individuality of its identities comes not only from variation in their external context but also from the differing arrangement of their internal components. Think of the compound as a bouquet of flowers. Each of its identities is analogous to a photograph of a different arrangement of those flowers. No two arrangements are exactly the same. There is no "sameness" in Mind—no duplication.

In Biblical language, each generic idea is an idea "whose seed is within itself." Man, beast, and plant reflect the qualities of parenthood, yet Mind remains the actual cause and creator. Parenthood and childhood qualities are simultaneous effects. Neither is logically prior to the other.

The identities of certain comprehensive ideas represent so much of intelligence and life that these individual views appear to humans as separate minds. Individualized consciousness, however, is always an effect and not a cause. Therefore individualized views do not actually become separate minds in the strictest sense. There is always only one Mind.

The largest idea individualized by Mind is not star, planet, or earth. It is the compound idea man. Generic man expresses all the masculine and feminine qualities such as strength, compassion, intelligence, tenderness, justice, appreciation, courage, beauty, and purity. This spectrum represents the full image and likeness of the Father-Mother Mind. Thus, in Genesis, the full view is not recognizable until the "sixth day" in the ascending scale of larger, more comprehensive views—that is, not until all the component ideas have been recognized and appreciated.

VII—Complete, Consistent Creation

Mind's overall view of itself is restful because it is both complete and self-consistent. The completeness of each idea in Mind necessarily includes the correlative fact that its defined absence or theoretical opposite is unreal. This is the law of double negation; from this is derived single negation which figures in the process of abstraction (explained in chapter 5 and in the Appendix).

The overall view reveals the active equipoise of unfolding being. In the Bible's words, "And God saw everything that he had made, and, behold, it was very good."

5 Interpreting the Infinite System

The Limited View

Of all the ideas in the infinitude of Mind, the largest idea that Mind multiplies into individual identities is its own image called man.

> So God created man in his own image; . . .
> male and female created he them.

These spiritually complete identities are instances of Mind's thought in action. The universe exists as Mind's thought. Descartes' famous bedrock conclusion, "I think, therefore I exist" (a conclusion by which he reversed his descent into skepticism) bears closer relationship to our view of a mental universe than the 17th century forefather of modern philosophy probably intended.*

---

*Descartes was arguing for the existence of a separate, completely real physical universe alongside of spiritual reality. In other words, his view was dualistic.

Generic man is Mind's self-expression of its own thinking process. Each individualized representation of this reflected image called man, is no less than an instance of Mind bringing into focus its compound and prime ideas. The prime ideas are primitive, and yet they can also be thought of as abstractions from the compound ideas. Likewise, the compounds can be thought of as composites of primes. Each idea expresses both individual status and compound status simultaneously—primality and abstractness. Mind is thinking of all its creation at once; everything is always in focus now. The abstracting and compounding coexist simultaneously in the whole view.

As a corollary to Mind's abstraction process, man reflects this process—this capacity to abstract ideas from their context. He focuses on certain ideas while putting the complementary ideas out of immediate attention. (The reader can verify that he or she is engaging in this activity this very instant.) Along with *compounding*, *abstracting* is essential to thinking. Since the entire universe is one grand compound idea, thinking about anything amounts to letting the compounding and abstracting process be mirrored in our view of consciousness. There is nothing unusual in this selective focus any more than there is in our visiting an art gallery and centering our attention on one painting at a time. Of course, when a rational person visits an art gallery, he does not so lose himself in any one work of art that he forgets where he is. As we focus on particulars, we retain some awareness of their larger setting. We normally do not forget that we are concentrating on only a small part of what exists.

We can now make an interesting deduction from our hypothesis. Axiom IV states that qualities are the elementary distinctions in Mind and that each prime quality is an element of primal awareness. It is nothing less than an "awareness" itself—the awareness of the very quality it itself is. We can conclude that the identities of certain qualities (those pertaining to animation) when abstracted from the whole view in such a way that their connection to the whole view is also out of view—that these identities can appear to be independent "awarenesses." While appearing to be self-existent "minds" separate from their source, they are, nevertheless, only a subordinate or *subconscious* part of an individualized view of consciousness.

This is illustrated by the way we sometimes find ourselves so lost in thought that we are oblivious to our physical surroundings. Part of our thought concentrates so exclusively on its immediate, narrow mental view that it seems to "turn off" the rest of the world. Our latent knowledge of the world still exists, however. Sleeping dreams help illustrate this. While dreaming, part of our awareness temporarily* wanders within its own immediate view, appearing to itself to be detached from our larger, conscious selfhood.

Our complete selfhood always understands that any incomplete view is just that—merely a sub-conscious view restricted to the point of being hypothetical. One's entire conscious identity does not lose sight of the forest while examining, by abstraction, the individual trees. This is somewhat confirmed by the fact that when we sleep our overall identity continues to exist—ready to be recognized or "re-cognized" upon our awakening.

Entirely within a limited view or dream, things can appear quite different from what they actually are. For an imaginative analogy, consider how you can think

---

*The notion of temporariness is only a relative view. Every positive activity is happening right now, and there are no real separations to correspond to the finite notion of time. Within the nowness of reality time is only a relative measurement that compares limited views of this nowness with other limited views and not to the whole view.

about your automobile. Because you can think of the whole automobile, you are also able to think about its front half. There is no error in concentrating on merely the front half—as long as you remember that this is what you are doing. The automobile designer, the mechanic—almost any one of us—do this every day. But what if you are driving in heavy downtown traffic, and you begin to ignore the truth that there is also a rear half to your car? At this point you have changed a harmless, possibly useful abstract view into a dangerously incomplete view. This could entangle you in the further illusion that your fenders will remain unscathed even though you are driving in the very manner that one would who deliberately wanted to crumple his fenders.

As mentioned, an incomplete mental view can include enough qualities and exclude sufficient others that it appears *to itself* to be a temporarily separate individuality. The range of possible experiences for such "sub-consciousnesses" is the entire range of mortality including all possible dreams and impressions. The human experiences you and I are now having are exceedingly complex abstractions taken from our larger, real consciousness, which is a complete, individualized view of Mind in action.

To say that our human life is an abstraction sounds brash because we certainly feel that most of our experiences poignantly testify to concrete reality. But this mortal testimony is relative to the kind of frame in which we try to anchor our view. It is fairly evident that human opinions, beliefs, tastes, the feeling that time flies or drags, the permanence of material possessions—all of these are the interplay of but degrees of truth. We do get glimpses of enduring meaning, but often this meaning seems barely noticeable among the shadowy impressions that crowd our focus when we have our mental arena only dimly lit. And whenever we dim the light sufficiently—such that incomplete views of reality can be taken almost totally out of their real context—these incomplete views can become downright illusions.

Let's stretch our imagination to consider another hypothetical automobile, this time a silver sports roadster with wire wheels. It is night, the street lighting is dim, and a damp coastal mist is drifting in. We are across the street from the car, and all we see of it through the fog is two of the wire wheels and parts of the body. Suppose that due to the shadows and spotty lighting, all we see of the silver body is just enough patches and strips to form the exact pattern of a motorcycle frame. The effect is just as if a cold, wet motorcycle, beaded and dripping with dew, is parked under the yellow street light. But by our hypothesis, we know that there is no motorcycle; it is an illusion. And yet the wheels, the tires, the metal, and the silver paint—all of this is real. Everything we see is actually there—everything except a motorcycle. The overall illusion exists because it is a carefully edited, incomplete view of something that is real.

Three Degrees of the Limited View

Reality is the *infinite* system of constructive attributes. We now need to describe the full range of the *finite* view of reality by characterizing it under three headings which we will call three degrees of mortality.[1]

Third Degree

We start with the least limited view which we call the third-degree state of mortal thought. It is the most enlightened human view—limited just enough to qualify as human. This third-degree state is an ascending state whose mortality is about to vanish, swallowed up by its correlative wholeness in the way that faint shadows are swallowed up by total illumination. This state of thought easily recognizes the strength, love, beauty, and largeness of vision marking what is worthy and lasting on the stage of human history.

This third state of awakening is illuminated by qualities that enable it to discern the wheat from the chaff in experience. These illuminating qualities are neither too idealistic nor unrealistic. Humans cannot live and prosper without these qualities; and humans cannot but take notice of them because they are the light that delineates all experience—even our dark and fearful moments. Therefore every native tongue has names for most of the spiritual qualities that we can recognize. Since our present view is somewhat dim, the names are not always precise indicators. We cannot always tell from the name whether the reference is to a perfect quality or its almost complete, almost perfect third-degree expression or even its lesser, second-degree approximation. For example, consider the word 'love'—or the word 'truth.' The word 'truth' is a third-degree term because it applies to the absolute standard and to our highest sense of it. But we also use it to refer to the relatively highest standard as when we are expressing "honesty."

Second-Degree View and its Qualities

The word 'honesty' is a second-degree term because it refers only to the *human effort* to express truth. The human effort obviously falls short of the absolute expression of total truth which is an aspect of reality itself.

Truth is an attribute of Mind, and it belongs to our complete selfhood by reflection (axioms II and VI).

The same kind of distinction can be made between the other perfect qualities, which we see as third-degree states of mortal thought and their lesser, second-degree approximations. Consider these instances: purity versus temperance, love contrasted with affection, understanding as compared to faith and belief, joy versus pleasure, and spirituality as contrasted with humanity. The third-degree qualities are spiritual; the second-degree are moral. These moral qualities include hope, patience, meekness, bravery, reliability, compassion, friendship, and so on. Like the previously described "motorcycle," moral qualities are not fully real. The good that shines through them, however, indicates the deeper presence of something real and more valuable.

First Degree of Mortality

We now come to the intense degree of mortality—the first degree, which is a state of almost utter darkness. It comprises the negatives of experience such as hate, lust, greed, depravity, revenge, selfishness, sickness, error, death. These words do not refer to actual entities; they point to sharp contrasts—seeming absences of aspects of the one omnipresent substance, Mind. This is similar to the way that darkness is not an actual entity or substance; it is only the contrasted absence of light. To better understand this, we will now fill in the details involved in this claim.

The "Hole-in-Thought" Analogy

The first-degree mortal phenomenon has two phases. The first phase can be referred to as the "hole-in-thought" since no other terminology seems to be presently in use. The word 'hole' indicates the noticeable contrast between something substantial and its clearly demarcated absence. The sides of a hole define the absence—almost appearing to make it into something substantive in its own right. Nevertheless, a hole is only an emptiness defined by the material in which the hole appears. No matter how noticeable it is, it is never a substance of itself. (Someone might try to invent an exception, such as a hole within a hole that operates like a double negative, but such a case would only confirm the rule by illustrating its application in further detail.)

If we take a pine board that has a knot in the middle and punch out the knot, we then have a board with a knothole. We can see the knothole, point at it, and talk about it—as long as some of the board is there to surround the empty place. But if we cut away pieces of the board until every bit of wood is removed from around the hole, the hole will also vanish. Without its character-giving boundaries it is nothing.

The hole-in-thought is analogous. It has no identity except that which comes from its contrasting "sides" which are always "outside" of its emptiness. Without its defining boundary, the hole-in-thought would have no characteristics. The important point is that the hole-in-thought is neither substantive nor self-existent. The difficult thing to grasp is the concept of what serves as the defining "sides" for a non-spatial hole in awareness. The sides are the other ideas forming the immediate context of the specific quality that seems to be missing in our awareness.

The problem with our physical analogies is that the words 'hole,' 'boundary,' and 'sides' all suggest lines and surfaces occurring in space. But a hole-in-thought is not a hole in space. It is not analogous, in this respect, to a missing tile in a tile mosaic. But since physical analogies are the easiest to grasp at this stage, a good analogy would be this: If we think of fully illuminated consciousness as comparable to bright white light containing the full spectrum of colors, then the individual colors can represent attributes of Mind. Each color is located *everywhere* within the white light, and each color is a vital part of the whiteness. Likewise, each quality of Mind is everywhere present as a vital part of the total intelligibility of Mind. Now, in our analogy, if we block out with a color filter all of one wave length of light, say the blue wavelength, then the missing blue represents a hole that is everywhere in the formerly white light. The remaining colors, which are also everywhere in the light, are the sides of this hole.

This analogy is made sharper if the color filter is placed not in front of the light source but in front of the observer's eyes. Then the white light is still flooding the room—analogous to the omnipresence of Mind's attributes. The hole is now only an apparent one, apparent only to the observer behind the filter. It is nowhere in the room. Likewise, the hole-in-thought is nowhere except in the abstract hypothesis that thought can view itself separated from its completeness in Mind.

Individualized identities can view themselves at different levels of abstraction simultaneously. Each level is determined by how thought is focusing, that is, by how it is retaining sight of the complement of its focus or else abstracting itself from the connection with its complement. When it loses sight of the complete context and does so in such a way as to see an equal mixture of ideas and holes-in-thought, it can then begin to invert holes and real qualities. This is the second phase of the first degree of mortality.

Inversion of the Hole-in-Thought

The inversion is as if we were to confuse a photograph with its negative and unintentionally switch them. We would be reversing the roles of light and its outlined absence. The following two analogies will help us understand this mental process.

Suppose that you enter a dimly lit room. Across the room you see a checkerboard pattern of light and dark shapes against the wall. In the dim light it is difficult to determine whether the shapes are light-colored objects hanging in semi-darkness or dark objects suspended in half-light. You might choose the empty places to be the real objects while thinking of the actual objects as mere separating space. This would be an inversion, a switching of reality with its absence.

For a second analogy, suppose that you have a piece of carved marble statuary that you like, and for some reason you are making a plaster-of-Paris mold of it. After you finish the mold, what would the emptiness it encloses represent? The emptiness within the hollow plaster mold is the inverse of the original marble sculpture. This illustrates two important points concerning inversion.

First, this emptiness is absolutely unidentifiable by itself alone. Its ascribed identity is totally dependent upon the surface of the mold surrounding the emptiness. Second, the inversion of the sculpture is in every respect the exact opposite of the sculpture. To understand this, it is important to see that the volume of space in which the marble was extended is itself not the inverse of the statue. The volume of space has its boundary within itself just as the marble does, and this boundary has the same topology as the surface of the marble. Where the marble is concave, so is the space it formerly occupied.

The space is not an emptiness for it contains air, light, radio waves, and so on. But if we focus our attention on the purely abstract concept of *emptiness*, we then need to borrow a defining boundary (the inside surface of the plaster mold) to identify this emptiness as the absence of the sculpture. Here is where the opposites show up. Wherever the sculpture is convex, its theoretical absence is identified by concavity—the concavity of the mold. While the identifying surface is internal to both the marble and the mold, it is external to the emptiness. All the other qualities are also reversed. The marble's substance is inverted as the nothingness of the emptiness; the genuine translates into mere contrast; innate, self-existent individuality becomes borrowed identity. This is the process of inversion.

If the foregoing analogies are applied only to physical situations, they remain trivial because we rarely confuse physical objects with their absence—although in modern design we do find the interplay between physical materials and negative space often put to interesting use. But when the physical analogies are allowed to point to our larger mental landscape, they become significant.

Love

We will consider the suppositional inversion of the poorly understood attribute *love*. To consider love's inversion we must first consider love itself. Capitalize the word and it is a name for the one substance. Spelled without the capital, it is the name of one of the necessary primary attributes of that substance. Explicitly, love is the power to behold the loveliness of creation—the wondrous activity, life, joy, strength, grace, beauty, and intelligent individuality reflected by the people, creatures, and scenes we encounter. Love is basic not only to living things but to the structure of inanimate things too. Biological theories too often treat love as a mere secondary derivative of electro-chemical changes believed to constitute life. Or else they regard love as the disposition of complex forms to respond in certain ways to certain physical stimuli. Our theory goes deeper by presupposing love to be logically prior to the mental constructs called spacetime, matter, and physical energy.

Love is the creative force behind every truly successful endeavor. It is a light that reveals meaning in our daily round. It clarifies options and decisions, lifts the burden from our labors, and lets in joy. It helps us rise from the sorrows that sometimes seem necessary for our growth. To love is to express not only more life, vigor, and abundance, but more intelligence as well. We do not always think of love and intelligence as conjoined, yet the more love we can discern in a situation, the more intelligent relationships we can find there.

Consider the physician, manager, marketing consultant or elected official who is brought into a problem area to restore constructive activity. He or she will succeed to the degree that he or she has the appropriate form of love to bring to the problem. To a few, this light of appropriate love may appear disturbing in its directness. But the one who loves appropriately can see some good available right where its absence seems so prevalent to others. He or she will see better priorities, attainable goals, and immediate steps—even if these first steps be merely those of quiet listening or praying.

The Inversion, "Hate"

Now consider hate, the theoretical inversion of love. Hate is a state of thought looking directly at love and not seeing it. But instead of looking deeper, it focuses on this seeming absence defined by real background qualities. This is the hole-in-thought being inverted to look like something that is present on its own. Such inversions make a strong impression on thought that is poorly illuminated. Like an ugly shadow falling across our mental viewing screen, hate may cause us to react in alarm or horror. But if our mental home is sufficiently well illuminated, few shadows can be cast—at least few that look like anything but harmless, empty shadows.

We call inversions theoretical because they are grounded upon the supposition that we can see qualities apart from their source and then react to this supposition. Happily, to the larger view, the fraudulent inversion has no substantive power. Persons who have been caught up in hatred are often able to banish this seeming reality and its scars. How such steps of regeneration can become more visible and attainable depends first on mankind getting a better understanding of what is taking place in the mental realm.

Courage/Fear??

How do we know that hate is not the reality and that love is not merely the absence of hate? The question is slightly plausible. It would be more plausible if we were talking about courage, and someone asks, how do we know that fear isn't what exists and that courage isn't just a name for the absence of fear? The answer is twofold. First, if pursued to its logical conclusion, such an assumption would eventually require all we now consider negative—envy, jealousy, anger, ignorance, hate—to actually be positively performed actions rather than omissions. Their counterpart opposites—generosity, trust, affection, intelligence, love—would then have to be the omissions. The likely conclusion would be that the best way to build a successful business, coach a winning team, or direct a worthy performance would be to get people to *stop doing things*—to stop creating laziness, unintelligence, uncooperativeness, etc. But we know that the successful business entrepreneur, coach, or director motivates people to start doing things—to express more skill, teamwork, and so on. (This is quite different from the bizarre conclusion the philosopher Schopenhauer reached in the nineteenth century, namely, that the best situation for the world was the one with minimal life and activity.)

Second, in regard to courage and fear, we are being naive if we think that these are precise opposites. Courage is a second degree moral quality while fear involves the felt absence of much more than courage alone. Fear is the seeming absence of a host of real qualities including confidence, calmness, trust, inspiration, understanding, and joy—qualities vital to our general well-being.

No matter how powerful a tractor is for pulling up deep-rooted tree stumps from the farmer's pasture, the farmer can never use the tractor to pull up the holes left by the tree stumps. Holes have to be filled up—not pulled. Likewise, hate, revenge, fear, and so forth are not removed the way that realities are moved. The mental shadow and the inverted hole-in-thought are banished to their original nothingness only by our recognition of the specific hues of light that already fill these seeming holes. Even so, mental shadows are not to be treated frivolously because, to the thought troubled by the darkened outlook, they are frightening realities. But if we deal with them as ultimate realities, we will be apt to miss important clues on how to illuminate them out of our experience.

A surprising number of psychologists still accept anger and fear as natural, useful elements in our development—every bit as substantial and basic as love and confidence. Actually, these negative states should be recognized as warning signs that some area of our thought is losing sight of its natural capacity. When we are angry, we are trying to function without benefit of our normally apparent, whole, healthy consciousness.

No doubt we can envision narrow situations where the expression of anger might be the lesser of a given set of bad choices. Some kind of change may be desperately needed—the hypothetical alternatives being continued bondage, apathy, or suppressed resentment. Some therapists would encourage the patient to express anger, reasoning that this might loosen the mental log jam and restore the flow of new feelings. This would likely be an improvement; but, if we better understood such mental activities, we should see that one negative is not the thing that actually dislodges another area of darkness anymore than one error in arithmetic is the best means for correcting another error.

It needs to be emphasized that the level of consciousness where the mental chemistry of inversion takes place is not necessarily the recognizable level of everyday thought and experience. The recognizable level is only the effect. The causative level is deeper than our mere pictorial modes of thought in the same way that atoms and electrons are deeper than ordinary bricks and mortar. It would be a gross oversimplification to think that whenever we meet with resentment or fear that we are merely not seeing a large batch of appreciation, trust, or confidence. Our conscious and subconscious activities involve not only thousands of compound ideas and millions of their identities but also their translation into many levels of abstraction and inversion—all at once.

It is precisely because of this complexity of detail that the theoretically isolated areas of mortal thought can so easily invert what they do not quite see. The complexity allows the holes-in-thought to be so finely mixed with the qualities that they become hard to distinguish—like the tares and the wheat in the Biblical parable. The process is like the newspaper process for printing pictures with tiny dots and spaces. The finer and closer the dots and spaces, the more detail and realism is achieved in the pictures. And the more blurred the overall frame is, then the easier it is to confuse positive presence with its seeming outlined absence or negative.

Inversions and Opposites

It might be helpful here to recall something about inversions. Each generic type of inversion differs *in appearance* from every other generic type just as their counterpart real ideas differ *in a substantial way* from one another. Inversions are all the same in that they are defined absences or nothingnesses, yet they differ from one another because each represents the absence of a different attribute of substance. Some analogies might help here. A knothole is noticeably different from a donut hole, or a post hole, or the holes in Swiss cheese. At another level, poverty is noticeably different from ignorance, starvation, or boredom. And even deeper in thought and experience, hatred differs noticeably from envy and deceit.

I have been using the word 'opposite' as meaning the seeming *specific absence of*. Perhaps this needs elaboration. Commonly, we use the word 'opposite' in such sentences as "left is the opposite of right." This usage is correct within its usual restricted context but not in the total metaphysical context. "Left" and "right" are both directions, and, since the opposite of "direction" cannot be "direction," it therefore follows that the opposite of left actually is non-left (rather than "right"). In metaphysics this kind of distinction is most important. Only seeming absences can be the opposites of real attributes in an infinite system. A reality is never the opposite of another reality.[2]

Also, we should note that the noticeable opposite of anything is its *specific* seeming absence and not merely a *general* unawareness not sharply defined. Otherwise, we could say that because green cheese is not a direction, it is therefore the absence of the direction "left" and consequently green cheese is the opposite of left. The difference between general unawareness and specific nonawareness is illustrated by the difference between *all the things that never happened* versus a specific non-event such as that *it did not rain in Oregon yesterday*. The difference is in their defining contexts or boundaries.

6 The Structure of Spacetime

Time and Space

> To everything there is a season, . . . A time to be born, and a time to die:
>
> Whatsoever God doeth is for ever; . . . That which hath been is now; and that which is to be hath already been:
>
> —Ecclesiastes

Mind creates the vast array of identities comprising eternal consciousness. But our human sense of life discerns only some of these identities clearly—as clearly as if we were standing alongside them in the light. Many identities we do not notice at all. Others we see with variable clarity—as if we were seeing them in different stages of twilight or dawn. Of this variable group, some identities are sometimes detected through the process of inversion. That is, their precise absence seems to be what is present.

The consequence of all this is that, humanly, we recognize enough of reality to want to see more clearly its radiance, beauty, intelligence, and warmth in our lives. There are, however, some attributes that the human view cannot adequately discern until it drops almost all of its limits, the very limits that make it human. These attributes are the very ones of *unlimitedness* such as infinity, eternity, omnipresence, continuity, oneness, permanence, and so on. If we hypothetically consider what it would be like not to be conscious of these particular qualities relating to the infinitude of Mind, then we are considering the abstraction known as human thought. And because it is a hypothetical, limited view, human thought can react to its limitation and begin to invert infinity to where it is "taking notice" of its web of absences called "finiteness." Looking directly at reality's hereness and nowness, it notices instead a universe arrayed in separateness and impermanence.

Love, beauty, and most other qualities are humanly recognizable as valuable, creative forces, and yet they appear to be fleeting and fragile—as does life itself. To exist seems to mean having a location in a spacetime that serves as a separating function; wheres infinite substance operates as a uniting function. Mind differentiates without separating in any limiting way. Spacetime is a mental mode whereby we differentiate one thing from another by examining what is left after we have thrown out its infinitude. The remaining semblance of individuality is a kind of mental fragment called "occupancy of a unique portion of spacetime." From the materialist's view, love is thought of as enduring only in so far as we treat it as the abstraction romanticized in song and verse.

Ambivalent Values

Mankind, however, is not totally convinced of finiteness or materialism. Humans struggle with an ambivalent attitude toward physical tangibilities versus idealistic values. We often argue our need to give greater emphasis to one over the other. Regardless of which side we advocate, we are frustrated by our attempts to make direct comparisons between them. We make the comparisons anyway, as when pointing out to our children the advantages of having standards of character and conduct that outweigh predilections for immediate pleasure. All the while, we are uncomfortably aware that most of these comparisons are imprecise and thus a target for any clever person who cares to argue the other side. Men have not yet learned how to translate both the ideal and the physical to a comparable level. So man's scientific insight cries the need to come to grips with the reliability, provability, livability, and teachability of ideals.

Ideals lift us a giant step above the sensation-engulfed world of animal life. Even the materialist is apt to agree with the Biblical proverb, "Where there is no vision, the people perish." Who can doubt that hope, courage, wisdom, appreciation,—even "freedom and dignity" will not remain in our vision. While B.F. Skinner may disabuse these qualities when he feels we are taking them out of context with the larger reality (which he sees as physical), yet even Professor Skinner is promoting his own vision of mankind achieving the *freedom* to *dignify* behavior by intelligently selecting those environmental variables that reinforce better behavior.[1]

By reading Plato we can share many of Socrates' own thoughts about his trial before the Athenian Senate. But we cannot share his own physical sensations of these particular events. This suggests that time and distance are limitations more applicable to the physical level and not to our larger mental framework.

Life

What about life and death? Which level or framework do these pertain to? Is there any such self-existent state as death in an absolute sense? No, because death is a comparative notion or contrasting state—contrasting one temporal view with another. As such, it is built into the mortal view of life. Every mortal sense of finite identity appears to die. This merely means that its inversions are sooner or later exposed as having been dead all the time. They are defined as involving the seeming absence of life. Man does not die because his Principle which is Mind does not die. Only falsely defined states of consciousness seem to die because the mistaken definition shows its nature.

Interestingly, the Bible narratives show Jesus as rarely using the word 'death.' He went out of his way to give people a different view of what is happening. When he was told that the daughter of a man named Jairus had died, he said "fear not." When he arrived at the place where the mourners were carrying on, he said, "Weep not, she is not dead, but sleepeth." But, "they laughed him to scorn, knowing that she was dead." He then put the mourners out of the house and took the maid by the hand and called to her, "and her spirit came again, and she arose" (Luke 8:49-56).

When Jesus received word that his friend Lazarus was dying, he waited several days. Finally, he told his disciples "Our friend Lazarus sleepeth; but I go, that I may awake him out of sleep." His disciples misconstrued this remark, taking him literally and concluding that there was no serious problem after all. So Jesus had to tell them plainly (that, from their limited point of view) "Lazarus is dead." Still taking his time to get to Lazarus's home, Jesus finally arrived there—four days later. Eventually he called Lazarus forth alive from the tomb and told those nearby to loose him from his grave shroud and let him go. Jesus repeatedly taught his followers such things as "God is not a God of the dead, but of the living" and "The father's command is eternal life."* Jesus was equally disrespectful of the notion of time and space, saying such outrageous and infuriating things as "Before Abraham was, I am."

What Holds the Illusion Together?

There is a subconscious mental process that we all engage in that acts as a magnet in mortal thought, keeping it focused on illusions and keeping these illusions bound together as semi-coherent experiences. This false magnetism is nothing substantial. It is nothing more than an unrecognized fascination with the sameness of inversions. Mortal thought, seeing so many levels of individualized consciousness, unwittingly loses its bearing and becomes engrossed in comparing the sameness of the newly discerned *nothingness* its blindness "creates" to the already recognized nothingness it has been beholding. This process is a perverted use of intelligence because it distracts one's thought from its natural apprecia-

---

*I am indebted to the book *Jesus of Israel* by the Shakespearean and Biblical scholar Marchette Chute for calling specific attention to how the Bible records Jesus' view of life. The book, written primarily for young people and yet scholarly researched from the material available from Jesus' own time, is an uncommonly interesting account of Jesus' life.

tion of the uniqueness of Mind's attributes and their uniquely individualized identities.

For an illustrative analogy, imagine how we might be momentarily fascinated by a guest arriving at an important social gathering dressed identically as the hostess. We might find ourselves glancing at the guest, then the hostess, then back and forth again—confirming the sameness of their attire and comparing their reactions, whether of good grace or embarrassment. Our thought links the two people because of the sameness of their dress. But, of course, the link is more imaginary than substantial.

This "linking together" because of mortal thought recognizing "sameness" hints the subconscious reaction that is behind what is called mesmerism or sometimes animal magnetism. (Animal magnetism was the original term for what was later renamed hypnotism.) Occurring perhaps hundreds of times a moment in the darker recesses of mortal thought, this process makes it hard for humans to wrest themselves away from harmful habits or temptations. Even the seasoned Christian warrior Paul acknowledged how commonplace this problem is in human thought. He described its impersonal nature as "sin" when he wrote to the Romans when he was approximately sixty years of age:

> For the good that I would I do not: but the evil which I would not, that I do. Now, if I do that I would not, it is no more I that do it, but sin that dwelleth in me.
>
> (Rom 7:19-20)

Physical Sense

Total blindness, like total darkness, yields no sense impressions whatsoever. Partial mental blindness can yield a strange sense of perception—although we think of it as commonplace and normal. Follow, if you will, this explanation which begins with an invented analogy and then successively modifies it to come close to illustrating the mental process we seek.

Imagine someone who is color-blind to only the color red. His blindness does not merely make red things appear a nondescript greyish shade as in the usual color blindness. For him, red things do not appear at all. There is a complete blank in the field of vision wherever anything red exists. Our hypothetical person will see a flower garden the way we would see a nurseryman's catalogue with all of the pictured red blossoms neatly clipped out of each page. With this peculiar kind of blindness, our friend would still be able to point out red objects by merely pointing to the places where he did not see anything. But even though he can point to the red places, he himself does not know the nature of red or how it differs from blue or green.

Let us make the illustration more complex. Imagine that our friend has normal vision except for having the strange malady of becoming temporarily blind to the color he is focusing on at the very moment he focuses on it. This blindness only happens at the center of his vision, so that he can still see indirectly all the colors next to those he is looking directly at. We will also imagine that every distinct part of every object is a solid color. Now, as he looks at the world, it appears full of holes that come and go as he shifts his view. He sees the outlined absence of each thing he looks directly at; only indirectly, through his peripheral vision, does he see the real colors of the world.

We need to make one more modification. We will give our "blind" friend a hundred more eyes to go with his original two—since human consciousness is fragmented instead of being the single, whole eye that real consciousness is.

The end result is a kind of multitudinous "focal blindness." Our friend can get around fairly well in his world because he learns to deal with holes rather than objects. And from an overall standpoint he is at least faintly aware of all the colors and shapes. The only problem is that the more intently he tries to use his complex semisight (or semi-blindness) to pinpoint reality, the more he is led astray. The more he looks closely, the more he sees the opposites or negatives of what exists.

I believe that this analogy is not as farfetched as it may seem. It hints to what we are all doing. Perception is mental even though its grosser aspects can be characterized as physical sense. It is the addition of mental blindness (or the subtraction of awareness) that results in this strange, finite sense. Left to physical impressions alone, we would all be immersed in a sea of delusions. But happily, our reason and better education usually take the upper hand. Reason assures us the earth is not flat, the sun does not sail west, and Australians do not live upside down. At its worst, though, physical sense paints reality as half painful, ugly, and chaotic. We have yet to let our reason gain the complete upper hand and reveal to us the universe as an infinite system of vital qualities—more tangible, indestructible, and meaningful than ever described by physical sense.

There is an interesting account in Matthew, chapter six, of Jesus apparently speaking of how apt we are to slip into using mental blindness as our predominant means of perception:

> If the light that be in thee be darkness how great is that darkness?

A moment before this, he had given the remedy for this duality.

If therefore thine eye be single, thy whole body shall be full of light.

Jesus had been telling his listeners to lay up for themselves imperishable treasure rather than the corruptible treasure manufactured of physical sense impressions.[2]

Structural Matter

Mortal thought is aware of the imposing presence of this finite structure called sense impressions, although it does not see that the finiteness is subjective. The structure consists of multitudinous indirect glimpses of awareness defining areas of mental blindness. It is like a foam of millions of overlapping holes-in-thought. Because of its limited perspective, mortal thought unwittingly accepts this subjective self-awareness as objective reality. Wherever it looks, it contacts its own blindness. Acting as its own "sun glasses" screening out spiritual light, it sees everything tinted with finiteness. The grossest form of its perception is called physical sensation. When it summons more of the light of ideas, it begins to discern intelligible objectivity and cohesiveness in the discerned patterns. These patterns it calls physical law. But fundamental order or law is not physical; it is a-temporal and a-spatial.

Midway between gross sensation and more objective patterns, mortal thought perceives its structure as matter. This also ranges from gross to sophisticated—from ordinary clay, to the energy equivalence of $E = Mc^2$, to its analysis as collapsing spacetime geometry (described shortly). The more closely matter is examined from within its own premise that finiteness is fundamental, the more complex and contradictory it becomes. Its pallor of finiteness is composed of the blurred consciousness of overlapping outlines of blind spots within an indistinct reference frame. Nobel laureate physicist Werner Heisenberg wrote of how we begin to divide the world not so much as different groups of objects but as different kinds of *connections*. He said in *Physics and Philosophy*, "The world thus appears as a complicated tissue of events, in which connections of different kinds alternate or overlap or combine and thereby determine the texture of the whole."[3] While his overall point is different than mine, his description seems applicable here.

If we return for a moment to our built-up analogy about blindness, we can understand how it is that matter keeps changing its form. The perpetuation of mortal self-awareness depends upon continually changing the mortal focus. The reason is as follows: It is as if we were looking at a patchwork of thousands of colored squares through hundreds of synchronized eyes. As previously described, these eyes provide only peripheral vision because they are blind at the center of their focus. When we look directly at hundreds of the green squares with all the eyes, we see only the adjacent red squares. This is compensated for when we shift our focus to the red squares; now we see the green, or the blue, or orange, or so on until we go full circle back to the green. As long as we keep shifting our focus, we will obtain a useful overall representation of all the colors. (This "averaging" process corresponds to the probability function in quantum physics.) But when we try to pin down a specific color, we end up with a misleading inversion (corresponding to Heisenberg's indeterminancy principle).

Such a constant shifting of focus keeps the overall illusion "alive." But like the forbidden fruit—the knowledge of good and its seeming absence (evil)—, "In the day that thou eatest thereof thou shalt surely die." While matter seems substantial, its form is constantly decaying or wearing away. As flesh and bone, its cells are being continuously replaced by new material. When measured as energy, the thermodynamic law of entropy tells us that this energy is relentlessly merging into a homogenous, undifferentiated uniformity where no useful transfer of signal can take place. To sustain the constantly fading picture, a vibration-like shifting of our focus is required. Otherwise, the finite mental view will begin to lose its credibility and effervesce into nothingness just as ocean foam does when cast up on the motionless sand beyond the agitating surf.

Waves and Gravitational Collapse

A fundamental physical phenomenon described in almost all scientific theories (if one goes deep enough) is the wave phenomenon. Waves are alternating positive and negative states such as the crests and troughs manifesting the surface energy of oceans. Waves now are even recognized as propagating gravitation.

In the earlier mentioned physics textbook, *Gravitation*, by Misner, Thorne, and Wheeler (W.H. Freeman and Co., San Francisco, 1973) a number of formulas are given for the probability amplitudes of certain small-scale fluctuations in the electromagnetic field. The authors state:

> ...the smaller is the region of space under consideration, the larger are the field magnitudes that occur with appreciable probability. (p. 1192)

> ...the geometry is not deterministic, even though it looks so at the everyday scale of observation. Instead, at a submicroscopic scale it "resonates" between one configuration and another and another. (p. 1193)

> These small-scale fluctuations [$10^{-33 \text{ cm}}$] tell us that some-
> thing like gravitational collapse is taking place
> everywhere in space and all the time; that gravitational
> collapse is in effect perpetually being done and undone;
> that in addition to the gravitational collapse of the uni-
> verse, and of a star, one has also to deal with a third and,
> because it is constantly being undone, most significant
> level of gravitational collapse at the Planck scale of dis-
> tances. (p. 1194)

Distances at the Planck scale are fantastically small.
While the nucleus of the atom (approximately 10^{-12} cm)
is only one millionth of one millionth of one centimeter,
the nucleus is still 1,000,000,000,000,000,000,000 times
larger than the infinitesmal Planck distances in which
gravitational collapse and birth are described.

On page 1202 the meaning of this small-scale collapse
is further brought home to us. The authors state:

> No point is more central than this, that empty space is not
> empty. It is the seat of the most violent physics. The
> electromagnetic field fluctuates. Virtual pairs of positive
> and negative electrons, in effect, are continuously being
> created and annihilated, and likewise pairs of mu mesons,
> pairs of baryons, and pairs of other particles. All these
> fluctuations coexist with the quantum fluctuations in the
> geometry and topology of space. Are they additional to
> those geometrodynamic zero-point disturbances, or are
> they, is some sense not now well-understood, mere mani-
> festations of them?" (p. 1202)

The mathematical calculations regarding this infinitesmal collapse and rebirth yield a mass-density value
of 10^{94} grams per cubic centimeter. Considering that the
best recent estimates for the entire amount of matter in
the entire universe is 5.68×10^{56} grams[4], the above
density figure hints how much the physicality of the
universe is subservient to this mode of positive-negative
fluctuation. The physicist's description of these fluctua-

tions is, I believe, their translation into physical terms of the positive-negative mental fluctuations discussed earlier as the structural mode of mortal thought.

Philosophic Reflections

From our human standpoint, we look out on the universe's unfolding symphony of variety and majesty reflected in sunrise and starlight, in a friend's help, in a young child's laughing delight. We magnify these wonders in word, picture, and song. But when we try to assay such marvels by the yardstick of organized physical impressions (which are really mental), we end up tracing the sunrise colors to dust particles and diffused light and the friend's kindness and the child's joy to neurological reactions. Someday we will deal directly, as well as scientifically, with the vital qualities we now only dimly sense.

While light rays, particles, and neurological reactions represent patterns of order and symmetry, they side-step the direct apprehension of substance. Until we become willing to look directly at the attributes of infinite, mental substance, we shall be compelled to trace causality on and on in endless spirals—always finding one more sophisticated symbolization. Streaking photons, wheeling galaxies, multiplying chromosomes and replicating DNA molecules hint that mankind is awakening to glimpse the unifying Principle. The scientist's honesty and patience play a vital part in this dawning understanding. These qualities walk hand in hand with reverence for nature and a humility in the presence of nature's God.

If being is fundamentally an infinite, one-Mind system as put forth here, then research into the laws and wonders of the universe will also reflect itself in our advance in the art of living and self-government. Self-control will be recognized as an integral part of our natural freedom and protection under our governing Principle, God. Such progress will enable scientists, philosophers, and religionists to share a common vantage point from which they can still pursue their respective disciplines with a refreshing relevance to life.

7 Designing a Test of the Hypothesis

Increasingly we hear of attempts to measure not only the influence that physical acts have on mental processes but also the more remarkable influence that mental factors might have on physical processes. One type of experimental study underway is the examination of how an enriched, mentally stimulating environment for infants affects their future abilities and behavior. In a different direction, we hear of the attempts to measure the effect our thoughts and emotions may have on living plants. And popularized articles and books are appearing with accelerating regularity on parapsychological experiments involving extrasensory perception.

Most of these latter psychic forays, as well as the more established types of psychological studies, are based on the premise that consciousness is totally defined within a material universe. Other experimentors, more given to mysticism, are speculating that there is a mysterious conjunction of "otherworldly" forces from "inner space" with the physical forces of this world. Many inquirers are attributing causality to alpha waves and other equally physical phenomena. This research is undoubtably un-covering some useful information, but, if the theory pre-sented here is correct, the researcher's findings will be inconclusive as long as they see intelligence and sub-stance as basically finite. As an alternative, I suggest that an experiment be designed along the following lines.

The experiment is in two parts. The first part is in-tended as a preliminary test of whether or not it is possible for an individual to increase significantly his recognition of third degree qualities—i.e., to increase the spiritual quality of his thought and action. This is in preparation for the second part that will test whether such an increase can directly affect the so-called external world. The test will attempt to measure possible changes that can be brought about in some process at some distance from the participant's and observer's bodies. This will screen out any influence that emotions might have on one's own body.

A test of whether time is subjective to consciousness would be to see if a particular chemical process can be speeded up or slowed down. Could the rate that a certain number of grams of metal will dissolve in an acid be inhibited? And a test of whether the gravitational field (spacetime curvature) is internal to a larger field of con-sciousness would be to see if the pull of gravity on a standard mass can be altered sufficiently to show up on a delicate balance scale.

The principle participants would have to be trained for their part in the experiment. And the method of training would itself have to be developed through prior ex-perimentation. The goal of the training is to enable the student to increase his discernment of reality's attributes to the extent that he can clearly see (understand) the mental nature of so-called physical processes.

If he can clearly resolve the physical processes into their real background perception and inversion-dominated foreground, then he may be able to correct or replace these mental inversions with more enlightened and reliable perceptions. To do this, the researcher will need to bring to the foreground of thought useful qualities related to the physicalistic parameters in the experiment. By bringing flexibility, adaptability, durability, strength, and so on into clearer mental view he can demonstrate their effect on our perceptual-construction of the world we "live in." This will require that he get beneath the customary patterns of thought and observation (for these patterns are "creating" our familiar, material world).

If enlightened thought can, under controlled laboratory conditions, bring about the alteration of spatio-temporal processes, the likely conclusion is that our awareness of qualities supercedes so-called non-conscious (physical) existence. On the other hand, if substance is independent of consciousness, then changes in our understanding should have no effect on processes at some distance away.

The hypothesis being tested is that physical phenomena are a special category of mental phenomena—products of our limited perception and consequent misunderstanding of what is happening right here in the infinite system. Strictly speaking, this kind of test should not be characterized as a test of "mind over matter" since it is designed to test the effect of intelligent thought on less intelligent thought.

The test might require a number of principle participants. Objective standards would have to be developed for evaluating the progress (if any) being achieved by the participants in spiritualizing their thought—just as an athlete has standards for measuring his progress. This might require a method to score improvements in the participant's own well-being.

Along this line, a point that should be strongly emphasized is that the training should proceed in the opposite direction from using any kind of mesmeric suggestion or trancelike states of thought. Mesmeric states, whether self-induced or induced by an operator trying to hypnotize the student-researcher, are in opposition to this theory. The reason for this emphatic requirement is that hypnotism alters one's mental scenery by changing it in a negative way rather than a positive, healthy way. To draw an analogy, suppose you wish to eliminate an annoying shadow that falls across your breakfast room wall each morning. You would arrange to bring more light into the room or else remove whatever is blocking the already available light and causing the shadow. But the hypnotist's method is analogous to attempting to change the shadow into a more pleasing shape by blocking out more of the light. The result is a *larger shadow* and *less light*. Entering into states of mesmeric fixation or hypnotic sleep is not the way to awaken to a greater appreciation of one's own spiritual freedom under Mind's government.

Someone might voice an objection on the ground that sleep is a natural part of our biological cycle. The reply is that the spiritual quality hinted at by biological sleep is spiritual *rest*. And rest, in its spiritual interpretation, is not cessation or temporary loss of control. It is the dawning awareness of Mind's activity of being complete—that is, completely alive and well-balanced.

Besides ascertaining the truth for its own sake, the ultimate aim behind such a proposed test of the hypothesis that Mind underlies spacetime is not to control physical phenomena for our own material gain. It is to open the way for men and women to learn how to deal with the pressing problems and opportunities of our culture. For example, if the dismal statistics on employee theft and absenteeism, or on shoplifting and other kinds of misappropriation, could be altered for the better, the benefit would be more than a savings in material wealth. The real benefit would be the healthier attitude people would have toward themselves, their neighbors, and their jobs. The promising possibility is in improving the quality of human lives. Each individual deserves to taste fulfillment, to participate in excellence, to build something beautiful. He should be discovering something of the perfection inherent in himself and his life.

What seems to be needed first is a provable, fundamental understanding that can describe man so as to account for his intrinsic spiritual awareness on the one hand and the seeming existence of physical phenomena on the other. Toward that goal this theory is offered.

Appendix:
Eliminating the Paradoxes from Logic

I   AT ISSUE

The possibility of a new understanding of the role negation plays in language is a possibility that can have a fundamental impact on our view of logical systems. In particular, it could affect the applicability of the contemporary American logician Kurt Gödel's rather famous theorem on the incompleteness of arithmetic and other axiom systems rich enough to mirror self-referential statements.

This Appendix presents an analysis of negation which shows that the ability to make self-referential statements (and what are called impredicative definitions) is not the precise source of the so-called semantic and logical paradoxes as heretofore believed. These paradoxes have been a major problem for formal languages and systems such as the various types of set theory. This Appendix also shows how the notion of "provable sentence" (in a formal, deductive system) bears an equivalence relationship to the Tarski definition "true sentence" in that system. Thus the previously accepted disparity between the language that can define truth and the language that can define proof is not well founded.

In further consequence, an analysis of Gödel's first theorem is presented showing that, instead of proving the incompleteness of arithmetic, it actually points to a deficiency in *Principia Mathematica's* formation rule for handling the negation sign. A different formation rule involving a new, less restrictive theory of types is presented. If this analysis of Gödel theory is correct, it will vindicate the completeness of the axiomatic method.

Background

One of the quirks of language is the way we can use it to make self-contradictory statements that have an air of puzzlement to them. The most familiar is the paradox of the liar which has been known since the time of the ancient Greeks. An example of the liar's paradox is even given in the Bible by St. Paul, apparently unwittingly, when he alluded to a certain resident of Crete (the Greek philosopher Epimenides of Crete according to Russell):

> One of themselves, even a prophet of their own said, The Cretians are always liars . . . This witness is true.
> (Titus 2:12, 13)

But how can what the Cretian said be true if he is always lying?

Other examples of the linguistic or semantic paradox are:

((This sentence in double paranthesis is false.))

No negative proposition is true.

There is a male barber of a small village who shaves all the men of that village who do not shave themselves. Does he shave himself?

In this last example, it turns out that if the barber does shave himself, then it follows that he does not. On the other hand, if he does not shave himself, then he necessarily does,—clearly a contradiction whichever way we answer.

Logical Paradox

Apart from the harmless fun we can have with these amusing linguistic paradoxes in their many forms, we also find their close kin making a disconcerting appearance in formal logic and mathematics. This poses serious problems for the logician. Bertrand Russell made one of the major discoveries along this line in 1901. He was pondering what possible bearing Cantor's proof that there is no greatest number might have on his own program for tracing the foundations of mathematics back to pure logic. And in the back of his thought was the logical paradox of the greatest ordinal, published by Burali-Forti in 1897. Russell soon discovered that a self-contradictory class* could be derived from his logical axioms and rules of inference. This problematic conclusion was a severe setback which cost him another four

*The set of all sets that are "normal" (not members of themselves). Is it normal?

years before he was confident he had found a way around it. In the meantime, he communicated his discovery to Gottlob Frege in Germany—an almost unknown pioneer in mathematical logic, whose work Russell had been studying. Russell's letter had the effect of shattering the about-to-be realized hopes of Frege. Frege was just completing a long cherished labor in the form of volume two of his second major book on logic, *Grundgesetze der Arithmetik*, which he thought had finally navigated successful passage from mathematics back through set theory to safe anchorage in logic. Because of Russell's unsettling discovery, Frege subsequently gave up further major work in logic, writing relatively little else along this line. It was only after his death in 1925 that his monumental contribution to the development of modern logic really became well known. (Happily, this recognition was furthered by Russell's own repeated, favorable references to Frege's outstanding work.)

Russell's solution to the paradoxes, finally arrived at with the help of Whitehead in 1908 (after an abortive solution in 1906) was a theory of types. But it soon became evident that the theory of types was itself fraught with just as great a problem, and Russell admitted the same. Even sixty years later, in 1967, Russell stated that his and Whitehead's theory of types was only an ad hoc solution and never more than a stopgap.[1]

The Problem's Essence

There are three necessary characteristics common to the kind of paradoxes, both linguistic and logical, that we are discussing:

1. self-reference (historically associated with the semantic paradox).

2. definition in terms of a totality that presumes the existence of the thing defined. (Called impredicative definition in the literature and generally associated with logical paradoxes.)
3. negation (self-referential negation).[2]

My first major claim in this Appendix is that it is precisely the misuse of negation (characteristic three) that gives rise to the paradoxes. The misuse occurs because of a general misunderstanding of the deeper role negation plays in any ontology and language—including any formalized system that embraces the law of non-contradiction and the law of the excluded middle.* There is nothing amiss or harmful in totally self-referential statements or totally reflexive sentences of themselves. And they should not be excluded from languages—natural or formalized—for they are quite necessary on occasion.

Nevertheless, the literature over the past seventy years has emphasized that self-referential statements and impredicative definitions[3] are what bring on the paradoxes. Indeed, most of the ways suggested for getting around the problem have been ways to restrict impredicative self-reference. Whitehead and Russell's theory of types provided a characterization of a set as always one type higher than its members—whereby a well-formed set could not properly be a member of itself. In principle, this would prohibit us from considering such things as

---

*The law of non-contradiction tells us that a particular thing cannot both exist and not exist in one and the same specific instance; while the law of the excluded middle tells us there is no other alternative that to exist or not exist in any particular instance.

The first law tells us that no two sentences, one of which is the contradiction of the other, can both be true. Not (x & not-x). The second tells us that no two sentences, one of which is the contradiction of the other, can both be false. X or not-x.

the set of all sentences describable in general terms because such a set would also be describable in general terms and thus be a member of itself. (This gives rise to Russell's somewhat paradoxical claim that to legitimately describe a totality, we "must make any statement about the totality fall outside the totality."[4] This is a curious result, for we can ask, does a legitimate statement about the universe have to fall outside of the universe?—or even outside of all language?

Taking an altogether different approach, I will seek to show that the loose cog in the machinery of language and its syntax is the subtle way we sometimes try to use the concept of negation so as to violate its fundamental role in language. This failing sooner or later shows up in any language or system rich enough to allow the construction of totally self-referential statements.

Negation and its Positive Context

Negation is a simple concept founded on the notion of *noticed absence*. To negate something is to make its intended force become absent. To negate or prohibit an action is to insure that it remains absent from the domain over which one's authority extends. Regardless of the words used to express negation—'absence,' 'prohibition,' 'no,' 'not the case that,' 'false'—the concept can have meaning only in terms of a larger (or prior) positive concept or existential context. And any specific act of negation must have reference to something whose existence or meaning is already specifiable. This point is fundamental, and we need to understand it thoroughly. The simple fact is that negation requires a base which can support the concept before it can point to anything. And what it cannot point at is the very base supporting it—lest it negate its own foundation and immediately fall from sight.

Why is this? It is because the concept "the negative of" is a natural correlative to every conceivable existential except the totality of a primitive class. Every individual attribute or element of being, regardless at which level of abstraction it is described, includes the correlative that its absence (its "NOT-being") is NOT the case (at the level and instance where its being occurs). If you say that your name is George, you are at the same time asserting that it is NOT THE CASE THAT your name is "NOT George." That is, it is NOT "NOT George." This is the double negative. Amplifying this point, the existence of any thing implies that its absence is absent. That is, the concept of its absence is theoretical and not self-existent.

But if every existential implies its double negative, then one can ask, what is its single negative? The rest of this section and the next will answer this in detail; but, simply put, the single negative is part of the basis for our thought process of abstraction. Single negation is what we do to the immediate background of something in thought in order to consider the thing in the abstract. We consider its immediate context as theoretically absent. In other words, when we focus our attention on any one thing, we are abstracting the concept of that thing from its conceptual background. If we are studying the heart we think of the heart as it exists within the body, and we also think of it existing isolated as if on a pedestal. We make the concept of the rest of the body absent; we *negate* it from our immediate attention.

Light and Darkness

For an example (at the physical level of abstraction) of how the existence of something *must precede the concept of its absence*, consider "darkness." It turns out to be merely a name for a state of contrast, a state that is only definable in terms of the positive thing called light. The word 'darkness' refers only to the noticeable absence of light. We do not notice the absence in those instances where we would not expect light to exist in the first place. We do not describe the interior of a rock as being full of darkness.

Light is a "something." It has positive existence. (Even though we are considering physical light, the same thing would apply at other levels of abstraction. For example, mental *enlightenment* is also positive or existential when contrasted with ignorance or unawareness.) Scientists study physical light in their laboratories and postulate various theories about its existence and behavior. But no scientist is studying darkness or trying to invent a new kind of darkness for use in photography or in military operations. Light plays such an important role in our lives that we conveniently have a special term for its noticed absence. Similarly, we have special words for the noticed absence of other important things like air, wealth, knowledge, heat, honesty—special words like 'vacuum', 'poverty,' 'ignorance,' 'cold,' 'debt,' 'dishonesty.' Whereas, for less important things such as cottage cheese, we generally do not have special words to denote their absence. If, however, we were dependent upon cottage cheese for our very life and if it were frequently absent, we very likely would have a special word to denote its absence.

A person who is without any knowledge of light, could never have knowledge of darkness. This may be momentarily hard to accept, but a little reflection will show it to be true. The reason why people who have been blind all their lives know something about the meaning of the word 'darkness' is that they have already learned in various ways that there is something positive called light. The reverse, however, does not hold. A person can know about light without having to think of its noticed absence as a self-existent reality or substance.

Some Objections Met

Someone may raise the following objections to our claim that existence necessarily precedes absence or nothingness. First, he might claim that outside this expanding universe there is the void or nothingness surrounding this existing universe. Probably most of us picture the physical universe in just this way, somewhat like an expanding cloud of matter and gravitational force spreading outward into empty space. There are grave mistakes, though, in such an intuition if we think of the empty space as a *container* with some kind of objective existence.

First, there is no space or geometry outside of the universe—not even empty space. If there were, then that empty space would be part of the universe by definition. In the physicist's various recent models of the physical universe, space has no definable existence unless conceived as within the universe. In the expanding-universe model, it is not merely the distribution of the matter and energy that is expanding, it is space itself—the three dimensional field that expands as four dimensional spacetime. And the expansion is measurable only within the universe. "Outside" there would be no reference point from which to determine whether the universe were doubling in size every three seconds or shrinking. The expansion or contraction is relative only to something that exists, namely the universe's metric. And the universe's metric is intrinsic to the universe, not extrinsic to it.

Second, it makes no sense to claim that beyond something there is always the primitive nothingness *surrounding* it. The word 'surrounding,' in this case, has meaning only in terms of a logically prior something that is to be surrounded.

And third, the word 'nothing' has no ontological or

epistemological use except in terms of a logically prior "something." As the philosophers put it during the middle ages, *ex nihilo nihil fit* (out of nothing comes nothing).

(An objection raised by early Greek philosophers is mentioned in note 5.)

II SEMANTIC PARADOXES ELIMINATED

The second major claim of this Appendix is that it is meaningless to combine the sign for negation with a totally self-referential statement in such a way that reflexive negation would occur (if it could). Negation has no meaning unless defined in terms of some kind of relatively positive context. This context must be safely outside of the intended aim of the negation function (the argument in the domain of the negation function that the function inverts). In other words, in the negation function $f(a, \bar{a})$, the negation function 'f' inverts the argument 'a' in the domain of the function to '$\bar{a}$' (not a) in the counterdomain. What we cannot have is for f to be inside of its own argument a. Thus the following strings of words (group A) are, technically speaking, ill-formed at the deepest level of linguistic structure and thus meaningless.

A:
1. ((This sentence in double parenthesis is not true.))
2. (((This string of words in a triple parenthesis is meaningless.)))
3. I am now uttering a falsehood.
4. I do not exist.

The reason such utterances are ill-formed at the deepest level of linguistic structure (and thus cannot themselves assert that they are either meaningful or meaningless, true or false) is that the negation has not been used in a way that accords with the implicit rules deep within thought and language. At first glance, however, such contradictions may appear to be just as syntactically well-constructed as those in group B.

B:
1a. ((It is false that this statement in double parenthesis is not true.))
  b. This sentence is not written in English. (false but meaningful.)
2a. That string of words is meaningless.
  b. It is false that this string of words is meaningless.
3. I am not now uttering a falsehood.
4. The unicorn does not really exist.

Both groups follow the rules for using negation we learned in school; nevertheless, there is a fundamental difference between them. The four examples in group A have a construction that aims the negation against its own necessary base of support. To see why this is not allowable we need to look more closely at both negation and self-reference and their relationship to each other. The relationship will be explained by means of a new theory of types.

Logic textbooks usually describe negation as a *single-place* logical connective, distinguishing it from the *two-place* logical connectives 'and,' 'or,' 'if___then,' etc. Russell described negation as a function of one proposition. In a certain sense, however, negation is also a two-place connective even though it is a function of only one argument. It connects an element at an existential level with the *concept of its absence.* And this absence becomes a kind of "existence" at a contraposed level. This contraposed level may be thought of as the virtual shadow of the first level in that it is comprised of "outlines" that are the shadows or theoretical absences of elements at the first level. When using the connective "and", we choose both elements that are being connected, whereas when using negation we choose only one element; its counterpart "shadow" is automatically given us at the secondary level.

In spite of this automatic feature, it is still necessary that we choose a sentence structure that can accommodate the necessary separation of the levels. A totally self-referential structure will not accommodate the necessary separation. In a totally self-referential sentence the negation is aimed back on itself where it tries to invert itself, including its own base in the existential level. As already mentioned, some kind of existential background must define any absence and therefore must continue to be logically prior to the defined absence.

We can say that negation is the function that maps the set $\{1, \emptyset_1\}$* into itself to give us either $\{\emptyset_1, 1\}$ or $\{1, \emptyset_1\}$ but never $\{1, -1\}$ or $\{\emptyset_1, \emptyset_1\}$. These latter two sets violate the law of noncontradiction. But notice that the set $\{1, \emptyset_1\}$ has two members. These correspond to our two type levels.

Background for the New Type-Theory

Logicians treat both truth and provability as properties of sentences.† Sentences are considered true when they relate in a certain way to a domain of objects generally having existence or meaning beyond the "skeletonal meaning" (pure form) of the langauge. Sentences are judged true or false relative to models; we say that true sentences satisfy models of the language. The model can be considered a meaningful interpretation of the formal

---

*A subscript is applied to each empty set in this theory. This is explained in note 6.

†Sentences are formulas where the free variables have been replaced by definite names.

language, while the formal language itself is usually treated as a system of rules for combining uninterpreted symbols. (Just as arithmetic is a system of rules for seeing formal relationships existing between numbers, and yet the numbers can also be further interpreted to represent temperatures, prices, etc. in the domain of some model.)

Provable sentences, in contrast to true sentences, are those deducible from other well-formed sentences entirely within the formal structure of the language. This is the way assertions are proved in arithmetic or geometry. Provable sentences are called theorems, and all provable sentences in a consistent language are true. They comprise at least a portion of the true sentences in that language. The question is, do they comprise all the true sentences of that language or system?

Thus, an important question in mathematical logic about any given consistent formal language is whether all sentences that are true in the language are provable in that language. Gödel theorists have said no—not in languages with sufficient power of expression. This is because in these languages a self-referring sentence can be constructed (which says of itself that it is not provable) that turns out to be true because not provable and not provable on pain of creating a false theorem. And if a false sentence can be proven a theorem of the system, that system is not consistent. Kurt Gödel presented a proof in 1931 that showed this was the case with the arithmetic of the natural numbers and with any language rich enough to express number theory (and thus mirror the structure of self-reference). But Gödel theory is based upon the inference rules and formation rules relating to negation that are made explicit in *Principia Mathematica*. I maintain that one of these rules, namely primitive proposition 1.7 of P.M., is itself incomplete. It does not make explicit all of the fundamental requirements for using negation that are implicit in the other primitive definitions and assumptions axiomatized in P.M.

Whitehead and Russell admitted to this danger of having undetected presuppositions operating within their system. They write:

> But with regard to whether our premises "are sufficient for the theory of deduction", there must always be some element of doubt, since it is hard to be sure that one never uses some principle unconsciously. The habit of being rigidly guided by formal symbolic rules is a safeguard against unconscious assumptions; but even this safeguard is not always adequate. (*Principia Mathematica*, 2nd ed., vol 1, p. 90, Cambridge University Press, 1927)

Primitive Proposition 1.7 of P.M.

The sole formation rule in P.M. regarding negation is primitive proposition 1.7 (p. 97 ibid.) which states:

> If p is an elementary proposition, NOT p is an elementary proposition.

While this proposition could be an adequate formation rule for an arbitrary, uninterpreted, formal "game" involving the manipulation of marks on a piece of paper or noises uttered in sequence, it is not fully adequate once we start giving "NOT" its intended interpretation that we intuitively associate with negation in our daily speech. But admittedly, even then in the vast majority of sentences the formation rule as stated in P.M. would serve us adequately. But it is not adequate for those cases where the formula p is a simple* construction that can be

---

*By "simple construction" I mean the kind of directly self-referring statement as in the liar's paradox. But where p is a complex construction that achieves its self-reference through the use of a diagonal function or Smullian's norm function, then the negation is harmless when it sits outside of the structure. In the complex construction the negation has to be integrated into the repetitive nature of the structure in order to produce illegal self-referential negation. This is made clearer in section VI on Quine's analogy.

interpreted as referring to some essential existential characteristic of its own—such as its own truth in every truth-value model. And the authors of *Principia Mathematica* clearly had truth-value interpretation in mind, for they write:

> The system must lead to no contradictions, namely, in pursuing our inferences we must never be led to assert both p and NOT-p, i.e., both "p is a theorem" and "NOT-p is a theorem" cannot legitimately appear. (p. 13 ibid.)

They achieve this goal by introducing inference rules relating to negation and primitive definitions (p. 12, ibid.) involving negation. These bring into play the laws of non-contradiction and the excluded middle and their intended truth-value interpretation.

I am claiming that a new theory of types can remedy the incompleteness of primitive proposition 1.7 making it possible to state explicitly all of the formation rule regarding negation implicit in standard (i.e., two-value) predicate calculus.

The New Theory of Types

We assume for convenience sake the two-value deductive calculus with identity given in P.M. (exclusive of its type theory). And we also adopt Whitehead and Russell's convenient method of assigning truth values from the metalanguage to the formulas of the deductive calculus. We do this by assigning the numeral 1 to sentences of the formal language that are true in the metalanguage and the numeral 0 to sentences of the formal language that are false in the metalanguage (cf. p. 115 ibid.).

An intuitive idea of our type levels is that what we call truth in the largest model concerning our language is equivalent to type-level 1. This level is primary: its existence is logically necessary for there to be its derivative, the "shadow structure" called type-level 0. Level 1 is a conceptually self-existent unit. Level 0 has no self-existent unity. It is a piecemeal conception for it cannot exist as a full-blown totality. In other words, the negation function is a function that can look at only a portion of type-level 1 in any one operation. (This is analogous to the way we can conceive of a shadow only as the absence of a *portion* of all light. For, by definition, a shadow is outlined by light. The absence is at level 0 but the outline is always at level 1.) Furthermore, the negation operation is non-cumulative. That is, we cannot proceed to point out falsities in the universe and then reiterate this procedure until every relationship in the universe has been viewed as false—because this would mean our view is also false.

1. In every consistent model of a two-value logic there are two type levels. Call them type level 1 (corresponding to truth) and type level 0 (corresponding to falsity).

2. The negation sign is the logical connective relating the two levels.

3. The negation function inverts a formula from type level 1 status to type level 0 or from level 0 to level 1.

4. If p is a formula that does not have a structure that can be interpreted as predicating the essential requirement for its own type 1 status, then NOT-p is also a formula.

5. An even number of negation signs applied at the same level reduce to no negation while an odd number of signs reduces to a single negation.

(How this new theory of types would extend to number theory and set theory is presented in note 6.)

Everyday Speech

In everyday speech we do not rule out someone's intended meaning merely because he used poor grammar. The context in which his utterance occurs helps carry his message. For example, I can utter the words "I am not saying anything" and still convey meaning. Imagine that I am noisily clearing my throat, causing you to ask "what are you saying?" I reply, "I am not saying anything." You understand that what I mean is "I was not saying anything when I made those throat-clearing noises." If, however, we are programming a computor to receive a specific set of commands, then the computor will reject as meaningless any would-be command that departs in the slightest from our preestablished "grammar" or rules for the computor.

The point I seek to make is that self-referential negation departs from the preestablished formation rules laid down deep in human thought and language. These rules are not arbitrary from our human point of view. Rather, they are inherent in the deeper consistency of reality itself. Any use of language touches a part of reality's structure; and as we sense the consistency in this structure, we demand it more and more of our expanding view. Thus, we invite into our logic all of the rules describing the unity of reality. Included among these is the rule that the negation conceptual operation inverts an element from the existential level to its counterpart, type-zero level.

Meeting Another Objection

Various borderline cases may be brewing as potential objections in the thought of the reader. For example: ((This string of words inside the double parenthesis is not a sentence.)) Is it a meaningful utterance or not? In ordinary usage we can say it is meaningful and false. But if we want to make our analysis analogous to the rigor necessary in mathematics, (and, for purposes of analogy, we require meaningful statements to be well-formed sentences) we will have to say that it is ill-formed and thus meaningless. The negation, which requires two levels, will not fit into the single level structure created by the intended meaning of the other words. Such a structure causes the negation to double back and negate the essential selfhood of the sentence. The word 'sentence' in this example has the same power as the word 'true' in the liar's paradox.

III LOGICAL PARADOXES ELIMINATED

The kind of construction that produces Russell's paradox, namely, "the set of all sets that are not members of themselves" is also an improper construction. Once again, the misuse of negation violates its natural rule—although this time the violation occurs under more complicated circumstances. This time the self-reference does not occur until the moment the negation is introduced—at which moment the structure can no longer accommodate the negation operation.

Background

We note that in set-theoretic terminology, every set is a subset of itself. This is because "subset" (as opposed to "proper subset") means "*equal to* or else *part of* the set." While all sets are subsets of themselves, only a few sets qualify as being members of themselves. A set of fathers is not itself a father. Sets that are members of themselves are those that involve what is called impredicative definition. They define a totality of some impersonal trait that is also shared by their members. Such a set has the very same property that defines its members. Some examples are: the set of things mentioned in this Appendix (for this set is now also mentioned); the set of all things conceptual (for it is also conceptual); the set of all things valuable (for it is also valuable). So far, so good.*

Six Cases

Now consider six successively more complex cases terminating in Russell's paradoxical set. In particular, consider whether or not each case involves self-reference. (We do not assume Russell's type theory nor the axiom of regularity.)

case 1:   *a set that is a member of itself.*
It is described by a membership requirement that refers back to the set. This construction is, however, not totally self-referential because the description does not capture the kind of essential property that is the necessary basis for this and every set.

case 2:   *a set that is NOT a member of itself.*
Allowable for the same reason that case 1 is. To disallow this would be drastic indeed; it would destroy set theory as we now know it since almost all sets come under this description.

case 3:   *all sets that are members of themselves.*
This case is similar to case 1. The phrase "all sets" does look suspiciously like the description of an even larger parent set. But it does not necessarily refer to another set. Recall that there is a difference between an apple and the *set* containing an apple. Likewise, there is a difference between "all apples" and the "set containing all apples" and between "all sets" and the "set of all sets.'

---

*Some logicians may say, "not so!—for it is not clear that these are sufficiently well-defined sets." This is further discussed in note 6.

case 4: *all sets that are NOT members of themselves.*
This is essentially the same as case 2. The construction is skating on thin ice, however, because, as mentioned above, the phrase "all sets" looks suspiciously like the description of another, larger parent set. Strictly speaking, though, the construction has not fallen through the ice.

case 5: *the set of all sets that are members of themselves.*
Is this new parent set totally self-referential? Does it describe only its members and its own embracing of them? Or does it also describe a generic requirement that every set including itself must have in order to be a set. No; all sets need not be members of themselves.

Furthermore, if we restrict our analysis to the information appearing in the immediate description, we cannot even tell whether the parent set is required to be a member of itself.

case 6: *the set of all sets that are NOT members of themselves.*
Here we suddenly have a form of illegal negation. The negation is being inserted into a structure that becomes totally self-referential the moment the negation is introduced. And this immediately undercuts the negation's positive base which it needs in order to operate. What is happening is this:

The word "NOT" is being added to case 5 because the members of the parent set are now to be negatively described as "sets that are NOT members of themselves."

Since the member sets are described as including *all* sets having the negative property, this allness will also embrace the parent set if the parent set has this negative property.

But the parent set cannot help but have this property once the negation is introduced. This is because an inescapable, totally self-referential construction is created—namely the following biconditional:

(a) "This parent set is a member of itself *if and only if* it is NOT a member of itself."

Regardless of whether we conclude the set is or is not a member of itself, it will be captured by either one or the other alternative given in the contradictory biconditional. But let us see how the contradictory biconditional comes about.

It is a trivial logical truth in any language that employs a two truth-value logic that x is true *if and only if* x is true. By virture of this, we arrive at another simple truism pertaining to every set, namely that:

(b) "A set is a member of itself if and only if it is a member of itself."

This applies to every set—our parent set included. The left half of (b), "a set is a member of itself if," also applies to any parent set (i.e., a set whose members are also sets) because every parent set has the potential of being a member of itself. It might have the same distinguishing property that it requires of its members.

Also, the right half of (b) potentially applies to the members of any parent set because this side of the biconditional gives a membership property that could be the property distinguishing the member sets of any parent set. In case 6 the property is to be the inverse of case 5, and therefore the "NOT" is inserted in the description. But the description is doing double duty. It gives the membership requirement and it also is the right half of the trivial biconditional truism.

With the insertion of the negation into only one side of the true biconditionala self-contradictory biconditional is created which automatically captures the parent set by capturing all alternatives that are available for the parent set. Thus, the negation has caused the would-be set to be both self-referentially described and self-referentially negated. The self-referential negation causes the entire structure to now fall outside of the class of well-formed formulas employing negation.

Case 6 in Set-Theoretic Notation

The source of the problem that causes case 6 to appear to be well-formed is the way logicians have interpreted the axiom schema of abstraction: $\exists y (\forall x)(x \epsilon y \longleftrightarrow \varphi(x))$—literally: there is a y such that for all x, x is a member of y if and only if x has the property φ. (In plain English: "for every property, there is a corresponding set of all things having that property.)

This axiom schema had early been thought to produce a true axiom whenever $\varphi(x)$ is replaced by any formula in which only x is free. But this turned out to be an insufficient constraint on $\varphi(x)$ because, if one substitutes the negative description $(x \notin x)$ for $\varphi(x)$ and then instantitates for $\exists (y)$ to get $\forall x(x \epsilon b \longleftrightarrow x \notin x)$ and then supposes that b satisfies x, the result is $b \epsilon b \longleftrightarrow b \notin b$ which is a contradiction. One traditional way around this was to weaken the axioms by replacing the axiom schema of extension with Z e r m e l o' s   a x i o m   s c h e m a   o f   s e p a r a t i o n But this was done merely to avoid an obviously contrary biconditional and not to avoid meaningless self-referential negation which actually went unnoticed. It went unnoticed in Zermelo-Fraenkel set theory because (x∉x) of itself is well-formed and the self-referential negation gets buried under two successive substitutions taking place within the axiom of abstraction.

We need not weaken the axioms of set theory (as in Zermelo-Fraenkel set theory or in Von Neumann-Bernays set theory) if we weaken the formation rule for using negation by means of the new two-level type theory. This is less of a restriction on the formation rules than is the Russell-Whitehead theory of types.

The reason the new type-theory applies to set theory is that it clarifies the concept "property" (φ) and shows us that negative descriptions cannot always do the work of existential properties. There is no possibility whatsoever of creating Russell's paradox from the axiom schema of abstraction as long as φ is not a negative description (one controlled by a negation).

If we wish to abstract the negative of any property (the defined absence of a specific property) we can then use Zermelo's axiom schema of separation. This insures that the negative description and the set associated with it are definable from the "outside" by insuring they are a subset of another already established set. This avoids the danger of trying to use a negative definition or description as something that can exist of itself alone (without a logically prior positive context to support the negation function).

Semantic Paradoxes Revisited

We can now see that the aforementioned biconditional truism also applies to the structure in a semantic paradox in the following way: "This sentence is true *if and only if* this sentence is true." We can also see that what we have been calling total self-reference turns out to be expressible as a biconditional truism where (1) each half is identical in both its essential form and meaning to the other half and (2) each half makes reference to the total biconditional by saying *"this* biconditional," *"this* formula," *"this* expression," etc.

The "liar's" so-called paradox is really an ellipse of the biconditional, "(This sentence is true *if and only if*) this sentence is NOT true." So, once again, we see that the negation sign has been inserted into just the right half of a biconditional structure. This application of the negation function to only one side of a self-referential biconditional is not merely a matter of semantics; it is a matter of structure as well. In a very technical sense, "This sentence is true if and only if this sentence is not true" is not even a biconditional formula. It is a meaningless construction that is similar to the form of a biconditional.

The Formalist Program

The formalist program for studying logical systems (largely instituted by Hilbert) is an attempt to be scrupulously honest in keeping semantic interpretations separate from the syntax or formal structure of utterances. This has led to a heavy reliance upon the physical shape of strings of symbols as the best mirror of formal structure. But, quite possibly, deep grammar is allied to something more basic to human thought than spatio-temporal arrangement. From an idealist view in philosophy, I am arguing that formal structure is ultimately a matter of meaningful qualities in the same way that meaning is and that we best understand structure in the degree we discern the law-like relations involved—a long step from the spatial arrangement of marks on a page.

Relying on the physical appearance of symbols to mirror these relationships is practical only so long as we accommodate the manipulation of the symbolism to match the deep structure as well as the surface grammar. If the negation function does indeed involve more than our usual symbolism indicates—and likewise with the structure of the self-referring utterance—then we cannot dismiss these distinctions as merely semantical in nature. We will need more detailed symbols to reflect this complex structure. And if the theory of two type-levels does not readily identify with our present notation, we might remember that Russell's type theory also required the addition of new superscripts and subscripts to the notation. In fact, the complete notation was so cumbersome that the printer had to leave most of the symbols out of *Principia Mathematica*.

Consequences

Looking ahead to see what effect the elimination of the paradoxes from logic might have, we see two areas of research into the foundations of science that have partly been based upon the assumed existence of the paradoxes.

One of these areas concerns the "completeness" of the axiomatic method as a suitable foundation for discovering all the truths statable in a formalized system. This area is dominated by what is sometimes referred to as Gödel theory.

The other closely related area concerns the distinction between "truth" and "provability" as these concepts pertain to sentences in both natural and formal languages. Likely, the most influential work in this area has been that of the mathematician-logician Alfred Tarski. His definition of "true sentence" is widely accepted by the scientific community as both materially adequate and formally correct—as is his work on semantic and syntactic notions of definability, model theory, and a score of related subjects in logic and mathematics.

IV TRUTH AND PROVABILITY

Professor Tarski's definition states that for any declarative sentence 'p', *'p' is true if and only if p.* In other words, *"Snow is white" is true* (is a true sentence) *if and only if snow is white.* Tarski writes

> ... we are interested in what might be called the logical notion of truth. More specifically, we concern ourselves exclusively with the meaning of the term "true" when this term is used to refer to sentences ... Sentences are treated here as linguistic objects, as certain strings of words or written signs. (Of course, not every such string is a sentence.)
>
> "Truth and Proof" by Alfred Tarski, *Scientific American*, June 1969, p. 63

Professor Tarski's basic thesis in the article quoted from, is that a formal language adequate for use in science should have sufficient deductive apparatus to be able to define the concept of proof in that language but not sufficient richness to define the concept of truth as it applies to the sentences of that language. This thesis is based in part upon the capability claimed to be inherent in any "semantically universal" language—the capability of producing paradoxes. A "semantically universal language" is one that contains names for all its own structural parts and thus can refer to any or all of its own sentences. Tarski writes

> . . . we can even construct in the universally rich language what is sometimes called a self-referential sentence, that is, a sentence S which asserts the fact that S itself is true or that it is false. In case S asserts its own falsity we can show by means of a simple argument that S is both true and false—and we are confronted again with the antinomy of the liar. (p. 67,68 ibid.)

> Hence we conclude that the metalanguage which provides sufficient means for defining truth must be essentially richer than the object-language; it cannot coincide with or be translatable into the latter, since otherwise both languages would turn out to be semantically universal, and the antinomy of the liar could be reconstructed in both of them. (p. 68 ibid.)

Later on in the same article Professor Tarski writes

> We are now aware [because of an argument closely related to Gödel's proof of his first theorem] that there are sentences formulated in the language of the [mathematical] theory which are true but not provable. (p. 77 ibid.)

I do not claim to have disproved this latter conclusion (which will be discussed in the next section), but I believe I have shown his conclusion about semantically universal languages to be invalid because the so-called paradoxes are not the fault of the semantic richness of a language. Rather, they are the result of our failure to understand the deeper structure implied in the concepts of negation and self-reference.

V GÖDEL'S FIRST THEOREM

In 1931 Kurt Gödel, a young lecturer in mathematics at the University of Vienna, published a paper with the formidable title "On Formally Undecidable Propositions in *Principia Mathematica* and Related Systems." For several years prior to this, mathematicians had been seeking a proof that arithmetic and similar axiom systems were complete or essentially complete (capable of being completely axiomatized). "Complete" here means capable of capturing all truths statable in the system as provable theorems of the system. Gödel found a way of proving that arithmetic (and any other formally axiomatized system containing a sufficient amount of number theory to mirror the structure of self-referential statements) is incomplete. And what is more, his theory claims that such systems are *essentially* incomplete—regardless of how many new axioms are added. Furthermore, as a corollary (known as Gödel's second theorem) Gödel gave a proof to show that the consistency of a formal system adequate for number theory cannot be proved within the system. (Any proof must use rules of inference that are not available within the system and thus are just as subject to doubt as the original consistency they are helping establish.)

Professor Gödel's actual theorem on the incompleteness of arithmetic has been stated informally in many different ways, two of which follow:

> In any consistent formal system adequate for number theory, there exists a true but undecidable formula—a formula that is not provable and whose negation is not provable.

> Any consistent arithmetic in which self-reference is possible, and in which the set of Gödel numbers of refutable formulas is enumerable, is syntactically incomplete.[7]

On the assumption that our previous line of argument is correct in principle, we should at this point be skeptical that any consistent axiom system will allow this kind of permanent gap between statable truth and its proof. And we should be further on guard in learning that Gödel theory depends on the creation of a type of negated self-referential statement—saying, in effect, "I am not provable." This statement is, at least, indirectly related to the paradoxes.

Our intuition might suggest that the true statements possible in a formally axiomatized system or language will be equivalent to the statements provable in that system. In other words, we might suspect that every sentence about a system and utterable in that system is knowable as true of that system *if and only if* it is potentially provable within that system. This is not to suggest that "truth" is synonymous with "provability." It only suggests that a logical equivalence exists between them, namely, the biconditional "If true then provable and if provable then true." This still allows us to hold that the truth of a sentence is determined by the relationship of that sentence to the largest model, or class of models, that embrace the formal system. (This accords with Tarski's definition of a true sentence.)

On the basis of the above intuitions, let us examine the general method Professor Gödel used to construct his proof. (An excellent, fairly rigorous description may be found in the article "Gödel's Theorem" by J. van Heijenoort in *The Encyclopedia of Philosophy* (Collier-Macmillan, 1967). And there is a relatively non-technical background article entitled "Gödel's Proof" by Ernest Nagel and James Newman in the June, 1956 issue of *Scientific American*. This article was further amplified regarding the details of the proof—and the problem of consistency and completeness in formal systems—in their book *Gödel's Proof* (New York University Press, 1958, 1960).

Gödel's Essential Method

Gödel's original paper (although elegant in its straightforward brevity) is extremely technical—as are the subsequent versions of the proof by other logicians.

Gödel's own version has forty-six preliminary metamathematical definitions (expressed largely in the notation of symbolic logic) and several important theorems which must be mastered before one can proceed toward the main results. We shall avoid this rigor and confine ourselves to an overview of the key ideas behind the proof.

By using a method somewhat anlogous to that used in a previously attempted, but falacious, paradox by Richard in 1905, Gödel found a suitable way of mapping meta-arithmetic statements (i.e., statements about arithmetic) constructed within a logical calculus, into elementary arithmetic itself. The crucial statement to be mapped into the arithmetic turns out to be unprovable in arithmetic but nevertheless true in arithmetic. It is the self-referential statement that says in effect "this statement is not provable."

The logical calculus wherein the statement is first constructed consists of the first order* predicate calculus of *Principia Mathematica* (including identity and type theory) and Peano's axioms for the natural numbers. By using a number of ingenious ideas, Gödel showed how the expressive power of this calculus could be mapped into arithmetic by using a system of what has since been called Gödel numbers. These are a subset of the natural numbers that are compounded in such a way that they are always uniquely decomposable into their original factors. The Gödel numbers provide a means of cataloguing in the arithmetic the vocabulary of symbols, the axioms, formation rules, and the rules of inference of the calculus. The Gödel numbering also allows the catalogu-

---

*First order logic is a logic with sufficient expressive power to generalize over individual variables (but not sets of variables). That is, it can make statements of sufficient generality to use the terms 'all' and 'some'. And of course it can make any of the statements possible in propositional ("zero order") logic, which can refer only to specific cases or specific variables.

ing of every well-formed formula and every well-formed string or sequence of well-formed formulas. These sequences are proofs because they start with axioms and end with theorems.

From an overall view, we have three levels of language operating in the proof:

1. our metalanguage (English) with which we talk about the entire operation,
2. the formalized logical calculus (the predicate calculus of P.M.) within which we first formalize all the formulas in the proof, and
3. The object language, arithmetic, which embraces the system of Gödel numbers and into which we map the predicate calculus.

The masterful stroke in this cataloguing process was the way Gödel mirrored in the calculus the metalogical assertions he needed to make about the calculus. He did this by reducing the assertions to assertions about the relationships between Gödel numbers. For example, a statement that such and such a formula is a component of another larger formula could be mirrored in the calculus by the fact that a specific Gödel number is a factor of another specific Gödel number. The concept of "factor" then has to be shown to be representable in the calculus. This is done by giving the algorithm or recursive function for performing the factoring operation. The algorithm is itself a formula, and thus the entire metastatement is reduced to a logical formula in the calculus. This formula can in turn be mapped into the arithmetic by determining its Gödel number.

Definition of Proof

A necessary step in arithmetizing the Gödel sentence "I am not provable" is that of showing that the notion of proof as it appears in "x is a proof array" (Gödel definition number 44) and "x is a proof of y" (definition 45) can be represented in the arithmetic. This is done by showing that the above statements are related to primitive recursive functions that can be defined in arithmetic.

In a formal calculus (i.e., a system of logical inference) a proof is a finite sequence of well-formed formulas where the last formula in the sequence is the theorem to be proved. Each formula in the sequence must be deducible from its predecessors by means of the rules of inference of the system. A recursive definition of "x is a proof of y" involves listing the steps for generating all finite sequences x which end with the formula y. Of course it is impossible to actually list all the infinite series of such sequences. But in principle we could do this by giving the steps of the algorithm for generating the infinite series.

Adding Self-Reference

Another essential step in Gödel's proof was that of finding a way to make a formula about a proof into a self-referring formula. Gödel achieved this by means of what is called a diagonal function which substitutes the Gödel number of the proof into the proof's own inner parts in place of its free variables. By this method (if he wanted to) he could obtain a new Gödel number for a formula that says in the metalanguage rough translation "I am provable" or, more literally, "the Gödel number of this formula is the Gödel number of the formula that is the proof of this formula." As long as such a formula does not involve self-negation there is no problem.

Adding Negation

Gödel, however, was seeking to state the negative of "I am provable," and the negative he was able to obtain comes out roughly as "the Gödel number of this formula is the Gödel number of a formula that is provable if and only if its negation is provable." This assertion is, of course, not provable unless the system is inconsistent. Since P.M.'s predicate calculus was already presumed to be consistent, then by contraposition, neither the final formula (called 'G') nor its negation could be provable in arithmetic. And since G asserts this very fact of itself, logicians concluded it must be true in its number-theoretic interpretation.

In further consequence, they interpret the proof as showing arithmetic is essentially incomplete, that is, it is incapable of being completely axiomatized so as to be able to capture all its own truths as theorems.

What has gone wrong, it seems, is that logicians are too hasty in assuming the predicate calculus is consistent under the present statement of its formation rules. The reason this alternative has not been seriously considered before is that it has not seemed possible to derive both p and not p from the predicate calculus in any straightforward manner. Russell's paradox (which, in effect, yields "p if and only if NOT p") has been blamed on the extraordinary case involving impredicative definition, which in turn was blamed on the axiom of abstraction as first formulated by Frege (Axiom V in *Grundgesetze der Arithmetik*, first edition, 1893). And this seemed the fault of naive set theory. Russell's paradox should have been blamed, not on impredicative definition but on the rule for handling negation.

In other words, Gödel's proof bears out the fact that P.M.'s formation rules are incomplete and thus inconsistent in that they allow self-referential negation to occur. This inconsistency is mirrored in arithmetic by Gödel's method of mapping where it comes out in the open—just as it does in set theory. The Russell-Whitehead theory of types does not prevent the inconsistency from being mapped into arithmetic.

Breaching Another Defensive Claim

A rejoinder often made in defense of the Gödel formula "G" is that the formula is safely established in the arithmetic where it is immune to the various objections raised against its interpretation in the logical calculus or our larger metalanguage (e.g., English). In particular, it has been claimed that the structure mirrored in the arithmetic is "innocent" of our subsequent interpretations that it is self-referential. The interpretation only occurs, as it were, "after the fact." Professor Gödel says in a footnote to his proof:

> Contrary to appearances, such a proposition involves no faulty circularity, for initially it [only] asserts that a certain well-defined formula (namely, the one obtained from the qth formula in the lexicographic order by a certain substitution) is unprovable. Only subsequently (and so to speak by chance) does it turn out that this formula is precisely the one by which the proposition itself was expressed.
>
> (footnote 15, as reprinted in *Frege and Gödel*, edited by J. van Heijenoort, Harvard University Press, 1970, p. 89)

The difficulty with this argument is that the proof necessarily depends upon the correspondence that can be developed between the structure of arithmetic and the structure in the logical calculus. And the structure in the logical calculus cannot be totally divorced from its intended meaning in our metalanguage, English. If the formal symbols are to have a certain intended meaning at the start of the proof and the same meaning at the end of the proof and if the total result is to have some

meaning, then there must also be a continuous development of meaning in both the metalanguage and in the
calculus—parallel to the structural development in the
arithmetic. And this parallel development in the interpretation cannot be switched on, off, and on—on when
it accords with our purposes and off when an embarrass-
ing inconsistency arises.

In other words, if self-referential negation develops a
contradiction in the running interpretation, we cannot
simply close our eyes to the interpretation and switch our
attention to the formalism. Once we break the continuous
chain of meaning in the interpretation we are thereby
estopped from further relying upon the original intended
meaning we had given the terms. We cannot even interpret the final arithmetic formula as true—at least not
until we clear up exactly where and why the contradiction seems to be taking place.

VI QUINE'S ANALOGY TO THE INCOM-
PLETENESS THEOREM

Professor W.V. Quine of Harvard University has provided an analogy for explaining Gödel's incompleteness
theorem—an analogy where the chain of reasoning stays
in the metalanguage. He modifies the following version of
the liar's paradox, a version so designed that its "physical shape" fulfills its own description and thus produces
the self-reference:

1) "Yields a falsehood when appended to its own quotation" yields a falsehood when appended to its own
quotation.

He modifies this by substituting 'non-theorem' for 'falsehood' to get

2) "Yields a non-theorem when appended to its own quotation" yields a non-theorem when appended to its own quotation.

Professor Quine comments

> This statement no longer presents an antinomy, because it no longer says of itself that it is false. What it does say of itself is that it is not a theorem (of some deductive theory that I have not yet specified). If it is true , here is one truth that that deductive theory, whatever it is, fails to include as a theorem. If the statement is false, it is a theorem, in which event that deductive theory has a false theorem and so is discredited.

> "Paradox" by W.V. Quine, (*Scientific American*, April 1962, p. 96)

Let us examine this more closely. Utterance **2** is either meaningless (not a real sentence in a strict sense that I shall specify) or it is meaningful. If the latter holds, then it is either true or false. And if it is true, then it is either provable or non-provable. This may be diagrammed as follows:

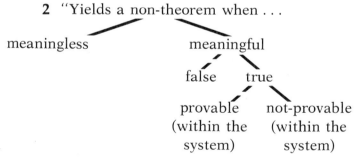

2 "Yields a non-theorem when . . .

meaningless   meaningful

false   true

provable   not-provable
(within the   (within the
system)   system)

Gödel theory claims that the most right-hand path gives the correct analysis of **2** whereas I argue below that the left-hand path indicates what has happened. (We will rule out the possibility of "meaningful but false" since this would mean we have a false theorem which would discredit the deductive theorem itself.) Therefore I must show that **2** is not well-formed (because of violating a subtle rule regarding negation) or else **2** shall likely continue to be accepted as true in a system wherein its truth cannot be proved as a theorem. This latter conclusion is analogous to Gödel's incompleteness theorem.

A Formal Language

For Professor Quine's example **2** to be analogous to Gödel's proof, it has to be treated as occurring within a rule governed language. His example is in English so English becomes our language, and we will formalize it by adding the proviso that each word we use is assumed to have only one agreed-upon meaning. Therefore, before **2** can be considered true, it first has to qualify as a well-formed sentence under the rules of English grammar. We will accept the customary statement of these rules in regard to the use of negation—our intention being ultimately to show that these rules, as stated, can lead to contradiction and paradox. (More specifically, our goal is to show that the rule for handling negation in natural languages has, generally speaking, not been spelled out carefully enough to reflect what we have called the natural rule for negation.) Our "formal" system's logic will be the full power of deductive reason which is based upon the meaning of words in language.

First, we look at **2** modified by removing the negation to give us

3) "Yields a theorem when appended to its own quotation" yields a theorem when appended to its own quotation.

This example qualifies as a well-formed sentence for it satisfies all the obvious rules of grammar and it cannot be accused of misusing negation since negation is no longer involved.

Next, in the spirit of P.M.'s proposition 1.7, we precede the whole of **3** with the negation phrase "It is not the case that" and obtain the well-formed sentence

4) It is not the case that "yields a thorem when appended to its own quotation" yields a theorem when appended to its own quotation.

We agree that **4** is well-formed (and lay aside the question of its truth for the time being).

The question now arises, that if the use of negation in **4** does not produce an ill-formed sentence, why should we believe it can do so in example **2**. To see why, we first note that example **2** owes its peculiar relevance to Gödel's proof not only because it speaks of its own "theoremness" or provability. It also owes its relevance to the fact that its self-reference comes as much from its form or "shape" as from the meaning of its words. In the familiar semantic paradox "this sentence is false" the self-reference derives almost entirely from the meaning of the word 'this.' But in example **2** the self-reference derives in large part from the peculiar repetitive form of the utterance which fulfills its own description. The appending of the phrase to its own quotation does the very thing that the phrase mentions. This placement of symbols so as to accord with their very meaning is slightly analogous to the diagonal function used by Gödel. It is certainly analogous to the norm function used by Smullyan in his version of Gödel's proof. When we take the negation out of **2** we have this kind of structural self-reference. And when we reapply the negation in **4**—only this time in front of the entire complex utterance—we are now merely performing the negation from a safe position outside of the scope of the self-reference. But in example **2** the negation is part of the repetitive description, and so it partakes of the self-reference that comes from the repetition.

Furthermore, the precise meaning of the term 'theorem' (or 'provable truth') is too closely allied to the meaning of the word 'truth' to escape the problem of paradox. Logicians generally agree that provable sentences are a subset of (i.e., less than or equal to) the true sentences in a language. It is the converse that is in question. With this in mind, we examine the two possible cases.

Case (A): if **2** *is provable*, then it is a theorem by definition of the word 'theorem,' and it is false by its own meaning. And therefore it is a false theorem. Thus, possibility (A) means that our grammatical rules allow contradiction and thus are themselves inconsistent.

Case (B): if **2** is *not provable* then it is true because it says it is not provable. And thus it seems that Quine's analogy does what he intended—it gives us a non-provable truth within our language and system of human reason. (And this is analogous to what Gödel's proof claims for arithmetic.)

But not so fast! It seems that, if anything, we have just *proven* the truth of **2**—contrary to the claim that it is non-provable. We have just given a proof that **2** is true by the means allowable in the deductive system of English language and human reason (*excluding* any spelling out of any detailed rule, natural or otherwise, for preventing self-referential negation). We have just compared the meaning of words to their performance in the structure and have arrived at the necessary truth of **2**.

Let us digress slightly from Quine's analogy while we discuss the notion of what serves as proof in natural language. Admittedly, the proof we speak of is wider in scope than that used in such subsets of language as the predicate calculus. These more formal systems require that we first group the meanings of our terms and formulas under symbols and then group the symbols so that they fall under the umbrella of various rules of inference such as *modus ponens*, etc. Using the larger system of human reason does not mean, however, that we are cheating. After all, the reason we have abstracted the more formal systems and use them is essentially to aid ourselves in seeing more clearly what happens when we are using the power inherent in ordinary human reason correctly.

In order for us to get the results from example **2** that logicians have thought we should get, we will have to arrive at their conclusion that example **2** qualifies not only as a sentence but that it is a true sentence. And we are expected to arrive at this latter conclusion by reasoning about what **2** says (or points to) and what its form does—in order to see if what it says about itself is the truth. This examination and analysis of the evidence is a deductive process and does not involve inductive inference. Furthermore, it should be pointed out that I am not espousing a "verification theory of truth" (the claim that the true statements are only those we have verified). I am merely saying that, in this particular example, we are expected to determine whether or not an asserted statement is true by means of our own reasoning about its meaning and performance. But this kind of deduction comes from no higher level than any other deductive proof performed within our "formal" system of rule-governed language and logic. We are not expected to accept the truth of example **2** as *being given to us from some "higher" metasystem.*

"Given" versus "Proven"

To illustrate what I mean, suppose you are working logic problems in class—problems that have been assigned by the instructor. The instructor gives you an arbitrary assignment of truth values for the sentential variables in the premises, usually such that the premises will turn out true. Then you work through the deductions required to solve the problem. When satisfied that you have demonstrated the rules of inference correctly and that your deduction is a valid one, you can then assign the truth value "true" to your conclusion. The initial truth value of the premises were *given* you whereas the conclusion was *proven*. If the given premises are axioms or theorems, then the conclusion is also a theorem or provable truth. Being *given* a truth value is clearly different from *proving* a truth value based upon what was already given.

In the example at hand, **2**, we are not *given* that it is true. We have to *deduce* this by use of the logic in human reason. The logic is the same as that we have just used to determine (prove) that **2** cannot be proven in case (A) without producing a contradiction.

The net result is that both (A) and (B) yield a contradiction; and thus they show a flaw in the ordinary formation rules of language which allow **2** and other semantic paradoxes to be considered well-formed. On the other hand, what I have called the natural rule for negation is not an arbitrary rule designed to get around these paradoxes. Rather, it follows naturally from the two type levels that reflect the fact that existence must be logically prior to defined absence.

VII CONCLUSION

A. Gödel's proof does not prove that arithmetic is *necessarily* incomplete (although this is exactly what it claims to have shown). Nor does it show an inherent limitation in the axiomatic method. Gödel's results do show that the predicate calculus needs a more rigorous statement of its formation rule for handling negation. This is necessary if we are to make the calculus consistent with the "natural rule" for using the concept of negation.

B.   Some mathematicians have said that the existence of certain unproven conjectures in mathematics, e.g., Goldbach's conjecture and Fermat's "last theorem," is empirical evidence that Gödel's results are correct. Others say the unsolved problems are of a different sort than Gödel's undecidable sentence of arithmetic. With this last view I agree to this extent: Gödel's proof is relevant only to a type of so-called self-referential "negative truth." It does not pertain to any other so-called "truths" except those that can be related, directly or indirectly, to self-referential negation through the two-level type-theory as explained in this Appendix and its Notes. The possibility exists that another axiomatization of the natural numbers—differing from Peano's axioms and embracing the new two type levels presented here—could provide the means to prove Goldbach's conjecture.[8]

C.   Regardless of claims made in this Appendix, the hypothesis presented in chapter four for our infinite system will still be immune from Gödel's theorem. This is because, under the axioms of the infinite system, existence is defined as that which is logically prior to the concept of absence. Therefore, self-referential negation is impossible. Furthermore, in the hypothesized infinite system, the largest model for defining "truth" is not a model that is separate or "disjoint" from the formal structure. The largest model is a system of elements that are *meanings*, a system which has its formal structure as one of its own proper subsets.

Notes

epigraph page

Albert Einstein—address at Columbia University, Jan 15 (year not given): *Essays in Science* by Albert Einstein. New York: Philosophical Library, 1955, p. 112.
Moses—Deut 33:27, *The Holy Bible*, Authorized King James Version.
Mary Baker Eddy—p. 468, *Science and Health with Key to the Scriptures* by Mary Baker Eddy. Boston: The Christian Science Board of Directors, copyright renewed by act of Congress, 1971.

preface

[1] One problem with George Berkeley's empiricism as a model for idealism is that for Berkeley the main entities with which the mind deals are "sensible things" or "sensible qualities" meaning physical sensations and physical sense impressions. These he also calls "ideas (borrowing this term from Lock). Berkeley did posit, in a vague way, another class of mental entities which he called "notions" and which are not sensed but rather are

"known by reflection." These "notions" appear to be a-temporal and a-spatial entities, but Berkeley never cleared up the duality this creates in his philosophy. (See pp. 79–81 of *Three Dialogues Between Hylas and Philonous* by George Berkeley; New York: Library of Liberal Arts/Bobbs-Merrill, 1954.

² An example of the growing recognition that a new concept of man is needed to solve today's problems is the study undertaken by the Stanford Research Institute for the Charles F. Kettering Foundation. The study concludes that humanity needs a new image of man to replace the "industrial man" concept that tends to measure human progress in terms of the economic growth of production and consumption. Policy Research Report 4, *Changing Images of Man*. SRI Center for the Study of Social Policy, Menlo Park, Calif. 1974. (Also reported in *The Christian Science Monitor*, Sept. 17, 1974.)

chapter one

¹ *Albert Einstein-Michele Besso Correspondence 1903-1955*, p. 538 (Paris, 1972). Quoted here with permission of the Estate of Albert Einstein. New York: Dr. Otto Nathan, Trustee.

chapter two

¹ The following explanation of "levels of abstraction" is the type of explanation that arises from the customary assumption that spacetime is primary to existence. Such a view suits our immediate purpose in this chapter since we are interested in the problems that arise out of accepting this point of view. This definition of "levels of abstraction," however, will hold up only so long as one doesn't press too hard at the meanings of the terms involved in the definition. When pressed too closely, a circularity will show up—as is the case in all theories of meaning wherein an ontology of physical objects and sense data is used to explain mental events.

An abstraction can be defined as a set of views or facts drawn from some larger population of views or facts. The abstraction occurs in the process of thought and also secondarily in such externalized forms as the recording of data in books, on blueprints, etc. (This definition is not meant to be rigorous since we have not defined "process of thought," "view," or "fact.")

A simple abstraction is involved in such a task as the ordering of uniforms for the university band. Someone would abstract an inventory of sizes from the domain of interest, namely, the facts about the physical features and preferences of the members (or potential members) of the band.

Another simple type of abstraction process is that performed by a biologist when he classifies members of the animal and vegetable kingdom into their phylum, class, order, family, genus, and species. He is participating in the successive abstraction of populations with common traits into smaller and smaller subsets that have greater similarity. He is dealing with two levels of abstraction—the level of individuals and the level of inclusive sets of which the individuals are members by virtue of their shared characteristics.

Abstraction reveals a structure that is less complex or less rich than the primary population from which it is abstracted. This is because abstraction intentionally overlooks information that is not of immediate interest. It achieves this by regrouping facts in "conceptual space"—the space in which we visualize sets, sets of sets, and so on.

The biologist's classification taxonomy is simple abstraction because both of his levels (his arbitrarily chosen individuals versus the sets of which they are members) come into view from slicing the "spacetime loaf" the same way. At the primary level we have a distribution of individuals in what we think of as real space. At the next level we have a view of these individuals regrouped in conceptual space. Both groupings, the individuals and the sets, are denoted by words that are classified as nouns.

Now, if we look at verbs, we find that we are examining a different slice of the spacetime loaf. Verbs, such as "to grow," "to run," "to smile," represent abstractions from a slice taken, so to speak, longitudinally through the "flow" of time (if we may use the analogy of time as a flowing succession of states). We tend to think of nouns as referring to spatially extensive, three-dimensional objects abstracted from a four-dimensional spacetime continuum. Thus, we think of "objects" as existing unchanged at a moment but as changing over time. With verbs, we tend to focus on phenomena not as objects but as events or processes taking place over time. Then we abstract from these changes the particular action-characterization denoted by the verb, e.g., running, climbing, etc.

The implication of this spatio-temporal approach to abstraction is that the more complex relationships between abstracted qualities produce such adjectives as 'tall,' 'hard,' 'rough skinned,' 'ripe,' etc.

Then, if we move on to combinations of even more diverse abstractions, we come to qualities that are far more complex *from the spatio-temporal point of view*. These complex abstractions now involve both the observer and his relation to the observable spacetime slices. The results are such adjectives as 'beautiful,' 'hazardous,' 'useful,' 'inspiring,' and so on. An entirely different approach to such adjectives is offered in chapters four and five.

[2] Regarding "existence" and the largest context with which one is immediately concerned, if a person's immediate concern is to stop a wave of thefts at school, the solution might be to put better locks on lockers. Such a step requires no deep theory— beyond common sense—and does not challenge any of our philosophical notions about space and time. On the other hand, if one's long-run responsibility involves finding an improved way to teach honesty in the schools, he will be concerned with the substantive nature both of honesty and of man's deeper nature. If the solution-seeker automatically assumes that traits of character have only secondary existence in respect to the primary reality of spacetime, he may be automatically and unwittingly blocking his path to the best long-run solution.

[3] The concept of "language games" is introduced by Ludwig Wittgenstein in his book *Philosophical Investigations*.

[4] Regarding *meaningful* questions, since the advent of Logical Positivism in the 1920's, meaningful declarative statements are generally considered to be ones that we would know how to verify, or else prove false, or at least know how to perceive some consequence of their truth. "How to prove" means how to do so in principle if practical means are not available. Thus, the statement, "the planet Venus is inhabited by little green people" is a meaningful statement even if incredible. But if the statement were to add "and the little green people are always

invisible and undetectable," then the entire statement would be meaningless. We no longer have any idea of what difference it could make one way or the other.

On the above basis, it is not hard to see why some skeptical philosophers have been tempted to hastily conclude that certain religious claims about eternal life or about God's real presence are meaningless. And the religionist's case has not been helped by religious people being guiltier than most of confusing their levels of abstraction. This is no doubt because of their greater exposure to ideas involving more than the physical level of abstraction. Furthermore, human thought often needs to rely on faith and inspiration when clear-cut understanding does not seem immediately available. St. Paul refers to this need when he chidingly alludes to "such as have need of milk, and not of strong meat."

⁵ Professor Quine's succinct summary of the ontological problem is quoted from p. 1 of "On What There Is," (from his book *From a Logical Point of View*. New York: Harper Torchbook/ Harper & Row, 1963).

⁶ I use the term 'persons' partly because Professor P.F. Strawson of Oxford University, in his book *Individuals* (presenting the case for the widely accepted view almost opposite of mine), accords "persons" (mortals) a more fundamental status among the primary particulars than he accords either their bodies, their behavior, or their thoughts. I agree that persons are fundamental among the particulars of experience, but I argue that this individuality goes much deeper than the mortal, physicalistic personality.

⁷ Philosopher D.C. Dennett, in his book *Content and Consciousness*, argues that mentalistic language is not fully reducible to the language of scientific physicalistic descriptions because different logics are involved in each. He seems, nevertheless, to be of the opinion that the material brain is the basis for human intelligence and that matter is primary in respect to the existence of life and consciousness.

⁸ Behavioral psychologist B.F. Skinner, in his book *Beyond Freedom and Dignity*, takes the approach that physicalistic de-

scriptions are much more feasible for developing a scientific technology of human behavior because they are more objective (their referent is more tangible). Even though I am taking almost the opposite approach, I nevertheless believe Professor Skinner has correctly pointed out the inconsistency of many traditional beliefs about motives and thoughts and other mentalistic descriptions. Traditionally, these mental entities are supposed to be operating in what he calls "autonomous man." And "autonomous man" represents a somewhat idealized human being who can act from the inherent worth, dignity, and freedom of his moral will. And this will is all too often supposed to be independent of the role that man's physical and social environment plays in shaping and reinforcing his behavior. I readily agree that there is an important correlation between the individual and his environment. The point I raise is that the environment and the person, perceived from the physical point of view, are both the *effects* of something much more basic. What we perceive as physical phenomena are perhaps no more the cause of changes in other physical phenomena than the moving images on a motion picture screen are causing each other's animation.

Professor Skinner proposes that the effective way to improve our social behavior is not to try to directly alter minds or thoughts or even to directly alter behavior itself. Rather, he suggests we focus on changing or developing that part of our environment that conditions and reinforces *desirable* behavior. As important and practical as this method may be (we use it much of the time—although probably not anywhere near to full advantage), still its underlying theory invites us to repeat the "autonomous man" type of mistake of which he warns us. The theory does this by presupposing an *autonomous spacetime environment* existing "out there" external to and prior to consciousness. This seems to be just as presumptuous as the older assumption of autonomous human "freedom and dignity" independent of environment or context.

[9] See Appendix for a discussion of Professor Kurt Gödel's famous 1931 paper "On Formally Undecidable Propositions of *Principia Mathematica* and Related Systems."

[10] It seems that physicists and philosophers create somewhat of

a paradox in using the word 'principle' to describe *ultimate uncertainty*.

¹¹ Dr. Heisenberg writes:

> The knowledge of the position of a particle is complementary to the knowledge of its velocity or momentum. If we know the one with high accuracy we cannot know the other with high accuracy; still we must know both for determining the behavior of the system. The spacetime description of the atomic events is complementary to their deterministic description." . . .

> Therefore, Bohr advocated the use of both pictures, which he called "complementary" to each other. The two pictures are of course mutually exclusive, because a certain thing cannot at the same time be a particle (i.e., substance confined to a very small volume) and a wave (i.e., a field spread out over a large space), but the two complement each other. By playing with both pictures, by going from the one picture to the other and back again, we finally get the right impression of the strange kind of reality behind our atomic experiments. (p. 49, *Physics and Philosophy* by Werner Heisenberg. New York: Harper and Row, 1962. Quoted with permission.)

Dr. Heisenberg goes on to point out the real difficulty arises when one asks the famous question "but what really happens?" Then he goes on to show how the observation that is used to pin down what is happening to a frozen moment or a "fact" is highly subjective. Along this line, Dr. J.M. Jauch, Director of the Institute of Theoretical Physics at the University of Geneva, points out in his book *Are Quanta Real?* that the word 'fact' comes from the latin 'facere' which means *to make*. The implication is that "facts are not entirely given to us from the outside world." Rather, "they are also shaped and endowed with meaning and significance by the man-made conceptual reference frame. It is just as though we were saying "What do you *make* of it?" (*Are Quanta Real?* by J.M. Jauch. Bloomington: Indiana University Press, 1973, p. 71.)

chapter three

¹ Drs. Fred Hoyle and J.V. Narlikar, authors of *Action at a Distance in Physics and Cosmology*, have produced a quantum-electrodynamic theory without the "infinities." Their idea has

not been fully evaluated as yet. It requires abandonment of causality—the idea that influences propagate only into the future.

2 The reference from Einstein's letter of March 30, 1950 appeared in *The New York Times*, March 29, 1972 in a three-part series on Einstein's unpublished papers (copyright by the Estate of Albert Einstein and quoted here with the permission of Dr. Otto Nathan, Trustee, New York.)

3 Einstein wrote, "The incompleteness of the representation leads to the statistical nature (incompleteness) of the laws." (p. 316, *Ideas and Opinions*, by Albert Einstein, New York: Crown Publishers, 1954.)

4 Sir Edmund Whittaker said that the term "curvature" is misleading and an unfortunate metaphor. Mathematicians use it to refer to any space that is not Euclidean or "flat." He wrote:

> . . . curvature in the sense of bending, is a meaningless term except when the space is immersed in another space, whereas the property of being non-Euclidean is an intrinsic property which has nothing to do with immersion. . . . What the mathematician means [by curvature] is simply that the relations between the mutual distances of the points are different from the relations which obtain in Euclidean geometry. Curvature (in the mathematical sense) has nothing to do with the *shape* of the space—whether it is bent or not—but is defined solely by the metric, that is to say, the way in which "distance" is defined. It is not the space that is curved, but the geometry of the space. (*From Euclid to Eddington* by Sir Edmund Whittaker. New York: Cambridge University Press, 1948. Quoted with permission.)

5 Possibly some empiricists (akin to such Positivists as Ernst Mach) might challenge this by saying that the notion of matter is as much a "mental construction" as the notion of energy or spacetime geometry. The Positivist's notion of "mental" is closely related to the subjective nature of sense data rather than to the concept of ideas as mental "universals." My reply is that, while I do seek to show how matter is a mental construct, I also seek to account for the difference between such things as ordinary stones and imaginary stones, and—going a step further—

between these sort of impressions and such qualities as justice and hope. Without this kind of accounting, we would have done little more than rename everything as mental. We would still have to account for the difference between the "physical-*mental*" and the "mental-*mental*."

6   Commenting on the concept of "infinite numbers," George Cantor, the founder of the theory of transfinite numbers wrote in 1888,

> All so-called proofs of the impossibility of actually infinite numbers are, as may be shown in every particular case and also on general grounds, false in that they begin by attributing to the numbers in question all the properties of finite numbers, whereas the infinite numbers, if they are to be thinkable in any form, must constitute quite a new kind of number as opposed to the finite numbers, and the nature of this new kind of number is dependent on the nature of things and is an object of investigation, but not of our arbitrariness or our prejudice. (p. 74, *Contributions to the Founding of the Theory of Transfinite Numbers* by Georg Cantor. New York: Dover Publishers, 1955.)

7   A trivial objection to the claim that ideas are time independent would be to argue that an eighth century laborer would be unable to think of a modern jet airliner while he remained in the eighth century. This is met on two accounts: First, the jet airliner concept is a compound concept, and it is thinkable as long as its components are thinkable. Anyone could think of it who is properly introduced to the major component ideas. Second, the concept of a jet aircraft is not entirely a purely time-independent idea because it is, in part, a materialistic concept. While one can argue that the concept of a material object must presuppose the concept of spacetime, yet this argument does not necessarily apply to a fundamentally spiritual idea such as "love."

8   Non-Euclidean geometries were conceived, however, in Aristotle's day. See "Non-Euclidean Geometry Before Euclid" by Imre Tóth, in *Scientific American*, Nov. 1969.

9   There is a parallel to this discussion. In this century, physicists did away with the earlier, rather mystical notion of "action

at a distance" which lay at the heart of Newtonian physics. Scientists had long assumed that there was such a thing, in principle, as a rigid rod; and they also believed that a magnetic field or a gravitational field behaved as if acting everywhere "rigidly" or instantaneously. They believed that if one end of a rigid rod was suddenly moved, the other end would move simultaneously—and likewise with a magnet or a heavy gravitational mass and their effects. But this involved instantaneous action across distance, which, on closer examination, turns out to be an amazing notion. Largely because of Einstein's discoveries, the Newtonian concept of instant action at a distance was replaced with the notion of the wavelike propagation of action. Thus, the concept of time was brought into the picture and placed alongside that of space so that the two are conjoined. Whenever distance is involved in the causal relationship, then time must also be involved. This is just another way of saying that, from the physicist's point of view, motion must always be involved in any causal relationship.

Bertrand Russell, in discussing this subject, wrote in the early 1940's:

> Since Einstein, distance is between *events*, not between *things*, and involves time as well as space. It is essentially a causal conception, and in modern physics there is no action at a distance. . . . Moreover, the modern view cannot be stated except in terms of differential equations, and would therefore be unintelligible to the philosophers of antiquity. (p. 71, *A History of Western Philosophy* by Bertrand Russell, New York: Simon and Schuster, 1967. Quoted with permission.)

The concept of motion seems simple enough—until one looks at it more closely; and then the old philosophic question of "what exactly is motion?" appears. The ancient Greek philosopher Zeno argued that motion and change were illusions. Russell comments on this in describing Zeno's famous paradox of the arrow in flight:

> Zeno argues that, since the arrow at each moment simply is where it is, therefore the arrow in its flight is always at rest. At first sight, this argument may not appear a very powerful one. Of course, it will be said, the arrow is where it is at one moment, but at another moment it is somewhere else, and this is just what constitutes motion." (ibid., p. 804)

Russell goes on to point out that there is a hidden difficulty within this so-called common-sense view of motion, for it turns out to have unwittingly assumed that motion is made of a series of discrete steps. And this is to assume that motion is discontinuous. Mathematics, he points out, resolves the issue. It shows us that in any series that is a continuum, there is never a "next position" in the series because between any two positions there is always an infinite number of intermediate positions. Similarly, between any two moments in time, no matter how close together, there is always an uncountably infinite number of intermediate moments. (The mathematical "moment" has no duration just as the mathematical "point" has no breadth and the line no width.

In mathematics, the notion of infinitesmals, used by Newton and Leibniz in their independent discovery of the "infinitesmal calculus" was, two centuries later, found to contain flaws, and was cast out of calculus by Cauchy and Weierstrass. These gentlemen paved the way to reestablish calculus on the rigorous foundations of the notion of a "limit." Interestingly, about a dozen years ago, mathematician Abraham Robinson of Yale University discovered how to make infinitesmals respectable again. (See, for example, "New Models of the Real-Number Line" by Lynn Steen, in *Scientific American*, Aug. 1971.)

Regarding action at a distance, it should not be overlooked that in our ordinary speech we have a way of referring to causation that is free of spatio-temporal ordering. We do so by speaking of "principle" and "law."

chapter four

[1] The Greek philosopher Xenophanes wrote (about 500 B.C.)) "God is one, supreme among gods and men, and not like mortals in body or in mind. . . . The whole sees, the whole perceives, the whole hears. . . . But without effort he sets in motion all things by mind and thought. . . . It [Being] always abides in the same place, not moved at all, nor is it fitting that it should move from one place to another." (*Selections from Early Greek Philosophy*, Milton Nahm, p. 85. New York: Appleton-Century-Crofts, 19964.)

The Greek Parmenides wrote, "Many signs in this way point to this, that what is is without beginning, indestructible, entire, single, unshakable, endless. . . . "the all is alone, unmoved, to this all names apply." (ibid. p. 93, 96)

² Regarding Spinoza's claim of explaining the unity of reality and the unreality of finite things, see, for example, pp. 255-257 of *A Student's History of Philosophy* by Arthur Kenyon Rogers. New York: Macmillan, 36th printing 1971).

³ On recent observations of scientists regarding the unity of mind and body see, for example, *New Mind, New Body* by Dr. Barbara Brown, of the UCLA Medical Center. Regarding the interrelationship between far reaching events, see, for example, *The Lives of a Cell* by Dr. Lewis Thomas, president of the Memorial Sloan-Kettering Research Center in New York.

   Drs. Fred Hoyle and J.V. Narlikar have developed a theory that "not only the inertial properties but the very masses of atoms have their origin in the farthest reaches of the universe. In other words, a proton, for example, has a certain mass because the matter in the rest of the universe has a certain distribution. As the matter in the universe changes, presumably the masses of atomic particles would also change." (Quoted from *Relativity and Cosmology*, p. 76, by William Kaufmann, III. New York: Harper and Row, 1973.)

chapter five

¹ My description of the limited view in terms of three degrees was borrowed from the description given in *Science and Health with Key to the Scriptures* by Mary Baker Eddy, pp. 115, 116, under the heading of "Scientific translation of mortal mind."

² David Hume, writing in 1739 on the relation of "opposite" said:

> But let us consider that no two ideas are in themselves contrary except those of existence and non-existence, which are plainly resembling, as implying both of them an idea of the object; although the latter excludes the object from all times and places in which it is supposed not to exist. (p. 15, Book 1, sect 5, *A Treatise of Human Nature*, David Hume, Selby-Bigge edition, 1896, 1951.

chapter six

[1] *Beyond Freedom and Dignity* by B.F. Skinner (New York: 1971).

[2] Matthew 6: 19–23.

[3] p. 107 of *Physics and Philosophy* by Werner Heisenberg, New York: Harper Torchbook/Harper & Row, 1962. Quoted with permission.

[4] For the estimate of the total mass of matter in the universe as 5.68×10^{56} grams see, for example, the article, "The Universe as Home for Man" by J.A. Wheeler *(American Scientist,* vol 62, Nov–Dec, 1974, pp. 683–691).

appendix

[1] Lord Russell made this comment to Mr. G. Spencer Brown. See *Laws of Form* by G. Spencer Brown, preface to the First American Edition, p. ix (New York, 1973)

[2] The negation may not always be obvious—as, for example, in Cantor's paradox of 1899 that the cardinality of the power set of the universal set is greater than the cardinality of the universal set itself. Here the negation is embedded in the concept of a set as both a collection and as the container for the collection. As a "container" the set acts as the complement of the collection defining the collection "externally."

[3] An "impredicative definition" is a definition of an object in terms of a totality of which that object is a member. For a discussion of impredicative definitions and set theory see, for example, the chapter "Predicative vs. Impredicative Conceptions of 'Set'" in *Philosophy of Logic* by Hilary Putnam.

[4] Whitehead and Russell write in *Principia Mathematica*, p. 38,

> The terminology 'all propositions' must be in some way limited before it becomes a legitimate totality, and any limitation which makes it legitimate must make any statement about the totality fall

outside the totality. *Principia Mathematica*, 2nd ed., vol. 1, Cambridge University Press, 1927)

[5] In ancient Greece, the Eleatic school of philosophers puzzled over the apparent paradox inherent in predicating *"not* such-and-such" of something. Plato saw part of their problem. He answered in the *Sophist* that "is not" does not mean "does not exist." It means "is other than." He went on to argue that if we say something is not beautiful, "not beautiful" is not a name for nothing, but a name for all things other than those that are beautiful. Our claim is compatible when we claim that negation is dependent upon logically prior existence. "Being" is a substantive state whereas "not-being" is only a state of contrast that requires reference to the state of being to provide that contrast. Being is self-existent, but not-being is no more self-existent than a shadow.

[6] The concept "set" involves more than meets the eye. A set is commonly defined as a collection where the things collected are the members or elements of the set. The existence of a specifiable collection implies not only the identifiable existence of the individual member elements but also the identifiable existence of the collection as an entity in its own right.

The identity—or identifiability—of an apple is contained in the apple's very existence. But the set concept brings into play another approach to identification. This is identification of member elements by thinking of them as "the complement of their complement." Without fully realizing it, one of the things we do when we think of the set containing an apple is we think of everything else other than the apple as constituting the exterior boundary defining the apple. And then we think of everything other than this "exterior" as constituting the apple within the set containing an apple. This is like sneaking up on the apple without ever looking directly at it. Consider the set of real apples weighing fifty pounds apiece. We conceive of this set as a kind of "empty container" since it defines a theoretical member that has no known extension on planet earth.

This "container" aspect involved in the notion of "set" is further brought out by the fact that we speak of *an apple* and, in set theory, we also can speak of *the set containing that apple*. In set theory the two are quite different whereas if sets were just names for their collected members, there would not be this difference. Consequently, in set theory, there is a difference between *nothing* and *the empty set–the set (or container) containing nothing.*

The various extant set theories (e.g. Cantor's classical set theory, Zermelo-Fraenkel set theory, Von Neumann-Berneys-Gödel set theory, and even Quine's version of set theory) all hold that there is only one empty set and that this empty set is a member of every non-empty set. I argue that this is an oversimplification that actually ends up making set theory more complicated than it need be. This oversimplification comes about, first, from adopting the rule that says "sets are equal if they have the same members" and, second, from assuming that since nothing is the same as nothing, that every empty set must therefore be the same as every other empty set. While it is true that all empty sets have the same number of members—zero—, nevertheless, they can differ in their nature as "containers." The set of 19th century women Presidents of the U.S.A. is a different empty set than the set of 20th century Kings of France.

Applying our theory of two type levels to set theory, we see that type-level zero represents the level of empty sets or "outlined absences" of type-level-one entities. In our predicate logic, the negation function is the operation that inverts a type-level-one concept to its type-level-zero counterpart or theoretical absence. Thus, every distinct type-level-one concept has its own unique empty set. This is as we would expect, for a donut hole is a different concept than a knot hole.

Thus, I propose that a set be recognized as a dual description—a description of the set containing its would-be members and also a description of the members themselves. If these described members are non-existent in the interpretive model with which we are concerned (for example, the physical world), then the description yields an empty container, which we call an empty set. Every non-empty set will have at least one particular empty set as one of its members becaue each kind of type-level-one member will have its own type-level-zero counterpart. Thus, the set containing an apple and an orange will also contain both a "non-apple" empty set and a "non-orange" empty set as well as a "non-apple and non-orange" empty set.

The descending chain stops here since the inverse of a type-zero set is the original type-one set.

Every set—every dual container/member description—must be defined ultimately in terms of type-level-one existence. Either the container must have type-one existence, or one of its members must, or both must. It is impossible to have both the container and the would-be member existing at type-level zero. Russell's famous paradoxical "set" (the "set" of all sets that are not members of themselves) is not an actual set because it reduces both its *container* aspect and its *content* aspect to type-level-zero status. It makes itself just as non-existent as your shadow would be in a pitch black room at midnight. (The detailed explanation of the nature of Russell's paradox is given under case six of part III of the Appendix.)

Along with these preliminary ideas for a new set theory, the author is also examining the possibilities of a new axiomatization of the natural numbers that differs from Peano's axiomatization. One reason for considering a new axiomatization is that Peano's unaugmented axioms do not reflect the basic differences between even and odd numbers and particularly between even numbers and prime numbers greater than 2. Mathematicians have recognized that in terms of the multiplication operation, the prime numbers are the building blocks of the natural numbers. Concerning the additive properties of prime numbers, however, certain complications arise. These complications have prevented mathematicians from finding proofs to such problems as Goldbach's conjecture of 1742 that every even number except two equals the sum of two primes (the number one not being considered a prime).

The new axiomatization starts with the number one rather than with zero. Zero appears as the type-level-zero counterpart of the number one, which is at type-level one. All the other natural numbers are successors in the usual fashion. However, every even number also mirrors the alternating pattern contained in the theory of two type levels.

In the new axiomatization, zero can be used as a place holder in conjunction with type-level-one numbers or in conjunction with type level one elements in the interpretive model.

Intuition suggests that such a system as can distinguish between even numbers and prime numbers at the basic level (without the help of definitions in the predicate calculus) will provide the necessary toe hold for solving Goldbach's conjecture and other problems such as Fermat's last theorem.

[7] The first example of a statement of Gödel's theorem on incompleteness is from J. van Heijenoort's article "Gödel's Theorem" in *The Encyclopedia of Philosophy*, New York: Macmillan, 1967). The second example I owe to Professor Craig Harrison of California State University, San Francisco.

[8] Regarding a possible replacement for Peano's axioms for number theory see the last four paragraphs of note 6 above.

Bibliography

Alfvén, Hannes. *Worlds-Antiworlds*. San Francisco: W.H. Freeman, 1966.

Anscombe, G.E.M. *Intention*. Ithaca, N.Y.: Cornell Univ. Press, 1969.

Audi, Michael. *The Interpretation of Quantum Physics*. Chicago: Univ. of Chicago Press, 1973.

Baxter, Stephen. *Philosophy of Mathematics*. Englewood Cliffs, N.J.: Prentice-Hall, 1964.

Berkeley, George. *Three Dialogues Between Hylas and Philonous*. New York: Library of Liberal Arts/Bobbs-Merrill, 1954.

The Holy Bible: Authorized King James Version.

Brown, Barbara. *New Mind, New Body*. New York: Harper & Row, 1974.

Brown, G. Spencer. *Laws of Form*. New York: Julian Press/Bantam Books, 1973.

Cantor, Georg. *Contributions to the Founding of the Theory of Transfinite Numbers*. New York: Dover Publications, 1955.

Chomsky, Noam. *Language and Mind*. New York: Harcourt Brace Jovanovich, 1972.

Chute, Marchette. *Jesus of Israel*. New York: E.P. Dunton, 1961.

———. *The Search for God*. New York: E.P. Dunton, 1941.

Clark, Ronald W. *Einstein: The Life and Times*. New York: World Publishing Co., 1971.

Copleston, Fredrick. *A History of Philosophy*, Vols 4–8. Garden City, N.Y.: Image Books/Doubleday, 1964.

Crossley, J.N. and others. *What is Mathematical Logic?*. New York: Oxford Univ. Press, 1972.

Dennett, D.C. *Content and Consciousness*. London: Routledge & Kegan Paul, 1969.

Descartes, Rene. *Meditations on First Philosophy*. New York: Liberal Arts Press/Bobbs-Merrill, 1960.

Eddy, Mary Baker. *Science and Health with Key to the Scriptures*. Boston: Trustees Under the Will of M.B. Eddy, 1971.

Einstein, Albert. *Albert Einstein-Michele Besso Correspondence 1903–1955*. Paris, 1972.

———. *Essays in Science*. New York: Philosophic Library, 1955.

———. *Ideas and Opinions*. New York: Crown Publishers, 1954.

156 *Mind Underlies Spacetime*

_____. "Einstein's Unpublished Papers." In *The New York Times*, March 29, 1972.

Enderton, Herbert. *A Mathematical Introduction to Logic*. New York: Academic Press, 1972.

Feynman, Richard. *The Character of Physical Law*. Cambridge, Mass.: The M.I.T. Press, 1967.

Foder, Jerry. *Psychological Explanation: An Introduction to the Philosophy of Psychology*. New York: Random House, 1968.

Frege, Gottlob. *Basic Laws of Arithmetic*, translated and edited by Montgomery Furth. Berkeley: Univ. of Calif. Press, 1967.

_____. *Grundgesetze der Arithmetik*, 2 vols. Jena: 1893–1903.

Gardner, Martin. *The Ambidextrous Universe*. New York: Basic Books, 1964.

Graves, John C. *Conceptual Foundations of Contemporary Relativity Theory*. Cambridge, Mass.: The M.I.T. Press, 1971.

Gödel, Kurt. "On Formally Undecidable Propositions of *Principia Mathematica* and Related Systems." (1931) in *Frege and Gödel*, edited by Jean van Heijenoort. Cambridge, Mass.: Harvard Univ. Press, 1970.

Heisenberg, Werner. *Physics and Philosophy*, New York: Harper Torchbook/Harper & Row, 1962.

Henkin, Leon. "Truth and Provability"; "Completeness," both in *Philosophy of Science Today*, edited by Sidney Morgenbesser. New York: Basic Books, 1967.

Hoyle, F., and Narlikar, J.V. *Action at a Distance in Physics and Cosmology*. San Francisco: W.H. Freeman, 1974.

Hume, David. *A Treatise of Human Nature*, edited by L.A. Selby-Bigge. Oxford: 1896, 1951.

Hunter, Geoffrey. *Metalogic: An Introduction to the Metatheory of Standard First Order Logic*. Berkeley: Univ. of Calif. Press, 1973.

Jauch, J.M. *Are Quanta Real?* Bloomington: Indiana Univ. Press, 1973.

Kant, Immanuel. *Critique of Pure Reason*, translated by Norman Kemp Smith. New York: Macmillan, 1965.

Kaufmann, William III. *Relativity and Cosmology*. New York: Harper & Row, 1973.

Kleene, Stephen C. "Computability" in *Philosophy of Science Today*, edited by Sidney Morgenbesser. New York: Basic Books, 1967.

Kuhn, Thomas S. *The Structure of Scientific Revolutions*, 2nd ed. Chicago: Univ. of Chicago Press, 1970.

Linskey, L. ed. *Semantics and the Philosophy of Language*. Urbana, Illinois: 1952.

Malcolm, Norman. *Problems of Mind*. New York: Harper & Row, 1971.

Misner, Charles W.; Thorne, Kip. S.; and Wheeler, John A. *Gravitation*. San Francisco: W.H. Freeman and Co., 1973.

Nagel, Earnest, and Newman, James. *Gödel's Proof*. New York: New York Univ. Press, 1960.

———, and Newman, James. "Gödel's Proof," in *Scientific American*, June, 1956.

Nagel, E.; Suppes, P.; and Tarski, A., editors of *Methodology and Philosophy of Science*. Stanford, Calif.: Stanford Univ. Press, 1962.

Nahm, Milton. *Selections from Early Greek Philosophy*. New York: Appleton-Century-Crofts, 1964.

Pepper, Stephen. *The Basis of Criticism in the Arts*. Cambridge, Mass.: Harvard Univ. Press, 1945.

Piaget, Jean, and Inhelder, Bärbel. *The Early Growth of Logic in the Child*. New York: W.W. Norton, 1969.

Plato. *Euthyphro, Apology, Crito*. New York: Library of Liberal Arts/ Bobbs-Merrill, 1956.

———. "Four Stages of Cognition: The Line," chapter 24 of *The Republic of Plato*, Cornford Translation. New York: Oxford Univ. Press, 1945.

Popper, Karl. "Self Reference and Meaning," chapter 14 of *Conjectures and Refutations*. New York: Harper & Row, 1968.

Putnam, Hilary. *Philosophy of Logic*. New York: Harper Torchbook/ Harper & Row, 1971.

Quine, Willard Van Orman. *From a Logical Point of View*. New York: Harper Torchbook/Harper & Row, 1963.

———. *Methods of Logic*, 3rd ed. New York: Holt, Rinehart & Winston, 1972.

———. *Philosophy of Logic*. Englewood Cliffs, N.J.: Prentice-Hall, 1970.

———. *The Roots of Reference*. La Salle, Ill.: Open Court, 1973.

———. *Set Theory and Its Logic*. Cambridge, Mass.: Harvard Univ. Press, 1971.

———. "Paradox" in *Scientific American*, April, 1962.

Reichenback, Hans. *The Philosophy of Space and Time*. New York: Dover Publications, 1958.

Rhinelander, Philip. *Is Man Incomprehensible to Man?*, San Francisco: W.H. Freeman, 1974.

Rogers, Arthur Kenyon. *A Student's History of Philosophy*. New York: Macmillan, 36th printing, 1971.

Rogers, Robert. *Mathematical Logic and Formalized Theories*. Amsterdam: North Holland, 1971.

Russell, Bertrand. *A History of Western Philosophy*. New York: Simon and Schuster, 1967.

———. *Introduction to Mathematical Philosophy* (1919). New York: a Touchstone Book/Simon and Schuster.

———. *Principia Mathematica*, (see Whitehead, A.N.)

Ryle, Gilbert. *The Concept of Mind*. New York: Barnes & Noble, 1949.

Siu, R.G.H. *The Tao of Science*. Cambridge, Mass.: The M.I.T. Press, 1957.

Skinner, B.F. *Beyond Freedom and Dignity*. New York: Alfred A. Knopf, 1971.

Sklar, Lawrence. *Space, Time, and Spacetime*. Berkeley: Univ. of Calif. Press, 1974.

Smart, J.J.C., ed. *Problems of Space and Time*. New York: Macmillan, 1964.

Smullyan, Raymond. "Self Reference in Languages" in *The Philosophy of Mathematics*, edited by Jaakko Hintikka. London: Oxford Univ. Press, 1969.

Spinoza, Benedict (Baruch) in *From Descartes to Locke*, pp. 230–293, edited by Smith and Grene. Chicago: Univ. of Chicago press., 1940.

SRI, Center for the Study of Social Policy. *Changing Images of Man*, Policy Research Report 4. Menlo Park, Calif: Stanford Research Institute, May 1974.

Stanisland, Hilary. *Universals*. Garden City, N.Y.: Doubleday, 1972.

Stein, Lynn. "New Models of the Real-Number Line," in *Scientific American*, August 1971, pp. 92–99.

Stoll, Robert. *Sets, Logic, and Axiomatic Theories*, 2nd ed. San Francisco: W.H. Freeman, 1974.

Strawson, P.F. *Individuals*, Garden City, N.J.: Anchor Books/Doubleday, 1963.

Suppes, Patric. *Axiomatic Set Theory*. New York: Dover Publications, 1972.

_____. *Introduction to Logic*. New York: Van Nostrand Reinhold, 1957.

Tarski, Alfred. "Truth and Proof," in *Scientific American*, June 1969, pp. 63–77.

Thomas, Lewis. *The Lives of a Cell*. New York: Viking Press, 1974.

van Heijenoort, Jean, ed. *Frege and Gödel*. Cambridge, Mass.: Harvard Univ. Press, 1970.

Wheeler, John Archibald. *Gravitation* (see Misner, Charles).

_____. "The Universe as Home for Man," in *American Scientist*, vol 62, Nov–Dec, 1974.

Whitehead, Alfred North, and Russell, Bertrand. *Principia Mathematica*, 2nd ed., vol 1, New York: Cambridge Univ. Press, 1927.

Whittaker, Sir Edmund. *From Euclid to Eddington*. New York: Cambridge Univ. Press, 1948.

Wittgenstein, Ludwig. *Philosophical Investigations*, translated by G.E.M. Anscombe. New York: Macmillan, 1953, 1958.

Index